Advance Praise

"Few in public safety have the breadth of experience of Gary McLhinney. I have known Gary for much of my career in Maryland, first during his days in the Baltimore Police Department, then as he moved to leadership in several state agencies, and served a key role in the examination of corruption by a police task force. He has been a trusted resource for journalists."

— Jayne Miller, Investigative Reporter, WBAL-TV

"I have known and worked closely with Gary for more than 30 years. He is the rare professional who came through the ranks and is accomplished at every level. Gary McLhinney is an anomaly in American policing—a street cop, union boss and police chief all in one—and great at all of them. Gary knows policing and leadership from every angle. He is a voice to listen to and a career to emulate."

— Former Baltimore Police Commissioner Fred Bealefeld

"Gary has seen American policing from all angles: street cop patrolling the streets of one of America's's most dangerous cities, union leader protecting the rank and file officers and police chief leading an agency. He truly has done it all. This is a great read."

— Edward Norris, former NYPD Deputy Commissioner, former Baltimore PD Police Commissioner, former Maryland State Police Superintendent

Bleeding Blue

Four Decades Policing the Violent City of Baltimore

Shali ↵GAURAV,
It is great to meet
you tonight and I hope
to see you again.

Bleeding Blue

Four Decades Policing the Violent City of Baltimore

Gary McLhinney

with Kevin Cowherd

Apprentice
House Press
Loyola University Maryland

First Edition

Hardcover ISBN: 978-1-62720-375-3
Paperback ISBN: 978-1-62720-376-0
Ebook ISBN: 978-1-62720-377-7

Printed in the United States of America

Designed and published by Apprentice House Press

Apprentice
House Press
Loyola University Maryland

Loyola University Maryland
4501 N. Charles Street
Baltimore, MD 21210
410.617.5265
www.ApprenticeHouse.com
info@ApprenticeHouse.com

To my incredible wife, Karen Kruger,
the smartest and bravest women I have ever met.
Without your love and support, I never would have written
this book or become the person I am today.

I love you.

Contents

Foreword

Former Maryland Governor Bob Ehrlich

We live in a cynical time. Daily, Americans watch as so many of our long sacrosanct bedrock institutions are impeached, even degraded, by powerful interests that seek to "transform" America.

No American institution has been under more progressive attack than law enforcement. Indeed, not so long ago it would have been difficult to find even a single person of prominence willing to adopt a "defund the police" platform. But things have changed. Today, police at every level are convenient targets for abuse, objects of scorn per progressive influencers.

Against this backdrop comes *Bleeding Blue*, a book about one man's life in policing and law-enforcement and written by my great friend Gary McLhinney. But the perfunctory "great friend" does not convey the depth of our relationship.

Gary has been close to me and my family for the last twenty-five years, since my early days as a State Delegate in the Maryland General Assembly. During that time span, he acted as my policy advisor, fundraiser, confidante, and Police Chief. Through it all, he has exhibited the professionalism, ethics, and loyalty that are hallmarks of his stellar career.

Bleeding Blue will engage you. Here is first rate storytelling about real people doing real (often dangerous) things in the real world. Most of all, this good read will make you feel better about the people who wake up every day with your security in mind. Yes, dedication to duty still counts in this world—a point brought home to the reader on every page. What better tonic for those of us looking to restore faith in the America we love.

And so when your workday is done and you would normally tune in to catch up on the bad news of the day, do yourself a favor and pick up *Bleeding Blue*. You'll sleep better in the knowledge that the thin blue line still stands for something...

Bob Ehrlich
Former Maryland Governor

1.

A Victory for Victims Everywhere

The drab curtain in the Maryland Penitentiary death chamber slid back not long after midnight. Looking through a small glass panel, we saw Flint Gregory Hunt strapped to a steel table, a clear IV line running from each of his arms.

Convicted of killing Baltimore police officer Vincent J. Adolfo nearly 12 years earlier in a grimy alley on the east side of town after fleeing from a stolen Cadillac, Hunt wore an orange jumpsuit and a white Muslim prayer cap. He lay motionless with his eyes closed, awaiting the lethal injection that would end his troubled life forever.

The date was July 2, 1997. Karen Adolfo, Vince's 32-year-old widow, stood next to me in the dim light. Also with us in this tiny room was Bishop L. Robinson, the police commissioner when Adolfo was killed and now head of the Department of Public Safety and Correctional Services.

Another curtain separated us from the media witnesses murmuring somewhere off to our right.

"Is he sleeping?" one reporter asked.

"Has it begun?" wondered another.

A third witness, Jennifer Gilbert, weekend anchor for FOX 45 News, fleetingly recalled a psychologist's warning that what we were about to see was "outside the range of normal human experience."

Another reporter silently made the sign of the cross.

Up until a few days earlier, Hunt, a street hustler and ex-con with a lengthy criminal record for armed robbery, assault, auto theft and other offenses, had insisted that he be put to death in the gas chamber.

He claimed to want that gruesome fate—where the condemned man gasps for air, lapses into convulsions, jerks violently and bangs his head against the metal chair—to showcase the "violence" the state was willing to sanction as part of his "murder."

But ultimately the 38-year-old Hunt had had "a genuine change of heart," according to his attorneys, opting for the fatal dose of chemicals that offered—arguably, some would say—a more humane death.

Standing in the stifling room, I held Karen's hand, hoping my sweaty palm wasn't more of a gross-out than a comfort. As the president of the Fraternal Order of Police, the youngest in Baltimore's history and the first police officer to hold that position in over three decades, I had vowed she wouldn't be alone to watch her husband's killer die.

My presence was intended to be a symbol—a powerful one, I hoped—that she had the support of all the roughly 3,000 brave men and women in the Baltimore Police Department.

Vincent Adolfo and the former Karen Blank had been high school sweethearts, married only two years before Vince's fateful encounter with Hunt in the section of town known as Iron Alley. The years since had been almost unbearably difficult for the families of both the young cop and his widow, forced to endure endless appeals in state and federal courts—and the legal machinations of Hunt's defense team—as they sought justice for Vince.

Maryland Gov. Parris N. Glendening had made it clear he had no plans to interfere with the execution. The Supreme Court had also declined hours earlier to issue an emergency request for a stay. Nevertheless, when I picked Karen up at her home on Miller's Island that evening for the ride to the prison, both of us were nervous.

Somewhere, we thought, there might be a judge ready to issue a last-minute order for another postponement that would again prolong the suffering of Vince's loved ones.

As the state's oldest prison, built in the early 1800's, the Maryland Penitentiary in East Baltimore resembles nothing so much as a medieval castle, with its huge granite walls, looming turrets, majestic stone tower and Gothic Warden's House.

Traditionally, the state has kept the exact time of its executions secret until the last minute. This dates back to the early 1900's, when prisoners on Death Row were hanged and "curious mobs" would descend on the proceedings, as well as opportunistic photographers snapping pictures of the ghoulish scene and selling them to the public at large.

Parking in a secure area, Karen and I managed to avoid the media that was already gathering, as well as the anti-death-penalty protestors congregating on Madison Street.

Yet as we made our way to the death chamber through the

vast courtyard, where ribbons of razor wire glinted ominously in the moonlight, there was no avoiding the scrutiny of the inmates in the cellblocks above us.

Their cries—some angry, some plaintive, some plainly unhinged—rained down as we hurried along:

"Fuck you people down there!"

"The food here sucks!"

"Yo, we got rats everywhere!"

"Get me outta here! I'm innocent!"

Karen was stoic throughout; if she even heard the torrent of howls, she gave no sign. Bishop Robinson met us on the second floor of the building and escorted us to the witness room. Out of our sight, Hunt, who had converted to Islam in prison, was allowed to say a short prayer in Arabic in his holding cell before he was led by guards to the death chamber.

He was strapped face-up on the padded table and asked if he wanted to make a final statement. He said no. Within seconds, the execution—only the state's second since 1961—began.

There was little drama to what happened next, save for the sobering realization that a man was about to be put to death.

William W. Sondervan, the assistant commissioner of the Maryland Division of Correction and the only one in the chamber aside from Hunt, served as the execution commander.

On his signal, the first of the drugs began to flow into the condemned prisoner's veins. This was sodium pentothal, designed to render him unconscious. Twenty seconds later, Hunt was given the second drug, Pavulon, to paralyze his muscles. And 20 seconds after that, potassium chloride coursed through his system to stop his heart.

Suddenly, we saw Hunt's right index finger jut straight

out. Later, Karen would say this was his "trigger finger," the same one used to pump two bullets from a .357 Magnum into her late husband all those years ago. She wondered if this was a final taunt from Hunt, a final "Fuck you," even after he'd expressed remorse a number of times for what he had done.

After a few rapid breaths, Hunt's eyes fluttered open. The curtain closed. He was pronounced dead.

Through tears, Karen said a quick prayer to Vince: "I promised you this would happen. So you can be at peace now. We saw this through together." Soon she would tell me "the ugly feelings" she had held inside for so long had finally begun to lift.

When the execution was over, I took Karen to meet with family members, friends and supporters outside the penitentiary. The atmosphere on the streets was surreal, with grieving Hunt family members and anti-death-penalty protestors holding candles separated from the Adolfo family and celebrating members of the FOP, some of whom sang: "Na, na, na, na, na, na, na, hey, hey-yy, goodbye!"

"The people who said this wouldn't help me, and I wouldn't get anything out of it—they're wrong," Karen later told a reporter for the Baltimore *Sun*. "They didn't lose a loved one and then get to see a murderer be executed.

"I didn't know how I would feel (about it)," she continued. "I thought it was going to be this immediate thing lifted off my chest. It wasn't that immediate lifting away, but it was a sense of peace."

I was still processing my feelings at this point, too. Watching a man die had not unsettled me - I had seen plenty of death in my time as a patrol officer in a city that often seemed to be perpetually in mourning.

I'd seen two children drown in an old pool trying to save their dog. I'd seen a young couple killed in a car crash on New Year's Eve. I'd seen a girl who fell into a fire pit while drinking on Christmas Eve. And I'd seen numerous young men shot and killed simply for dealing drugs on the wrong street corner.

Still, I couldn't help thinking how peaceful the demise of Flint Gregory Hunt had been compared to the awful way Vince Adolfo was forced to leave this world.

Leaving the death chamber, I went to a news conference in another part of the prison with the other witnesses. There, to the assembled media assigned to cover the spectacle, I read a short statement Karen had given me earlier.

"The events of today, 'it began, "are not about vengeance, but about justice. Closure can occur today for the Adolfo family and the police officers of Baltimore City."

I tried to convey Karen's thoughts that none of us wanted to be here, that Hunt had caused this moment in time to occur—not Vince's widow, not "the system" and not the Baltimore Police Department.

There was no joy in seeing a man lose his life. There was a sense of comfort—maybe satisfaction is the better word—that the criminal justice system worked and that its core tenet, *justice*, was served. Too many times, in the cases of cop-killers and other violent offenders, it isn't. But that feeling was tempered by the fact that Vince Adolfo was no longer with us.

There are so many advocates for those convicted of committing the most heinous crimes, but very few for the victims. This was, in a sense, a victory for victims everywhere. Certainly, it was a win for the Adolfo family, and for all the police officers involved in this tragic case.

The killing of Vince Adolfo and the execution of Flint

Gregory Hunt would go on to have a profound effect on me.

Leaving the penitentiary early that morning, I realized I was never prouder in my life to represent cops. It was the best job I'd ever had. Are you kidding? President of the union representing the good guys? There were 3000 other police officers who wanted to be here. But they couldn't be.

I was their proxy. I was their voice.

Along with her brother Dave and her boyfriend Ron Vida, Karen went directly from the execution to Oak Lawn Cemetery in Baltimore County, where Vince was buried. In the inky darkness, they prayed and placed a string of glowing blue lights, symbolic of police officers everywhere, around his grave.

As for me, I ended up at a small gathering at FOP headquarters in the working-class neighborhood of Hampden. I was not much of a drinker. But I had a few—maybe more than a few—that night.

Early the next day, I was awakened by a phone call from one of my union brothers. Someone had spray-painted graffiti on the FOP building. It read: "Revolution is about finding a way or making one. Greg Hunt."

I was appalled that someone might see that after such a tumultuous night in the city's history. So I called a contact in the Department of Public Works. Someone came out right out and sand-blasted the graffiti away.

No, there would be no cryptic message on behalf of a cop-killer visible to the citizens of Baltimore as the sun came up.

Not on our building.

Not on my watch.

Looking after cops had become my whole life.

2.

"Real Police Work in the City"

I grew up in the Waverly section of North Baltimore in the 60's and 70's, an idyllic time to be living on 37th Street behind old Memorial Stadium.

Depending on the season, the columns of the tidy row homes were painted blue-and-white for the Colts or orange-and-black for the Orioles. Plenty of ballplayers lived in the blue-collar neighborhood and someone's dad was always an usher at the stadium, so getting into the games was rarely a problem.

As kids, my friends and I played stick ball, step ball and curb ball. We also had a nice side hustle directing stadium-goers to parking spots on the nearby streets, spots we blocked off through the ingenious use of aluminum lawn chairs.

For this service, we were paid the princely sum of 50 cents per car. When someone graced us with a dollar bill, we automatically assumed the person was a millionaire, and that his or her car was therefore deserving of extra-special attention.

My parents, Jim and Shirley McLhinney, had moved from western Pennsylvania to Waverly when Dad, looking for a job with better pay and more security than the steel mill at Fort Pitt offered, became a firefighter in Baltimore City. He was assigned to Engine 6 on Gay Street, one of the oldest fire companies in the country, and one of the busiest.

Yet no matter how busy it got, no matter how bone-weary he was after 12- and 14-hour shifts at the firehouse, Dad was usually heading off somewhere to a second job, like many firefighters of that time. He worked as a Good Humor man and on the loading dock at Sears. He also drove cars into and out of freighters at the Port of Baltimore, the top "roll-on, roll-off" cargo port in the nation.

Within a few years, though, two events occurred that convinced my parents the city was no longer a safe place to live.

The first was the deadly rioting in April of 1968 that engulfed Baltimore following the assassination of civil rights leader Dr. Martin Luther King. Protestors filled the streets and thousands of National Guard troops were deployed by then-Gov. Spiro T Agnew to keep order. After eight days of unrest, the grim statistics included six dead, 700 injured, 5,500 arrested, over 1,000 businesses looted or burned and nearly $14 million in property damage.

Even more unnerving to my mother and father was a murder that took place a couple of years later at the little confectionery store down the street from our house. The store was where adults went for items like bread and milk, and where kids went to buy penny candy and bubblegum. During a robbery that went awry, the owner of the store was killed.

That was the last straw for my parents. We soon moved to the suburb of Towson, where I graduated from Towson High and attended Essex Community College with the thought of becoming an accountant. But the thought didn't last too long. Instead, to no one's surprise, I started thinking about joining the fire department.

In addition to my dad, my older brother Tom had become a firefighter. My grandfather and all my uncles and cousins were firefighters, too. And ever since I was a little kid, I'd been interested in everything having to do with fighting fires.

Hell, I thought, *might as well join the family business. They'll probably disown me if I don't.*

Yet this turned out to be another thought that didn't last long.

In the spring of 1980, at the age of 19, I took the exam to join the Baltimore City Fire Department. This included an agility test at Memorial Stadium, part of which required applicants to climb a 30-foot extension ladder, ring a bell near the top, and come back down.

Piece of cake, I thought. *I got this.*

Yeah, I was a cocky bastard back then.

Too cocky. Because halfway up, the ladder started swaying like crazy. It felt like the thing was alive, like it was trying to buck me off. My brashness quickly turned to terror. I said a silent prayer: *Lord, get me off this damn ladder and I won't take this fucking job.*

Even before this, I knew I had an issue with smoke. I didn't even like to be upwind from a barbecue grill. Now there apparently was an issue with heights, too. Not a good combination if your job might require you to rush into a tall burning building to save lives.

I ended up scoring well on the test. But there was no guarantee I'd be selected, so I decided I needed a backup plan. Thousands of candidates took the test to be a firefighter; far fewer took the one to be a city police officer, considered a much more dangerous job. And since the police were doing walk-in testing at their headquarters downtown, I gave it a shot.

I did well on the written test, submitted to a background check and took the required polygraph test, too. A week later, a letter from the department arrived in the mail. Eagerly, I tore it open.

But the news wasn't good: I had been rejected. No reason was given, but I was determined to find out the cause. So was my dad. He had worked with a firefighter friend whose brother was a high-ranking official in the police department, and the official agreed to do a little snooping around to see why I'd been turned down.

Soon enough, my dad had his answer: your son smoked weed in the past.

This wasn't something I'd tried to hide on the polygraph test. I'd admitted that back in my high school days, my friends and I would get high on the weekends, just like millions of other young people across the country. There was no point in trying to keep that from any prospective employers, let alone the police department. But honesty was apparently not the best policy in this case.

I was surprised at the rejection letter, but not crushed.

OK, I thought, *can't be a firefighter and the police don't want me. So what's Plan B?* Stay in school and get an accounting degree, I decided.

Yet a couple of months later, out of the blue, I received a

phone call on a Friday afternoon that would change the course of my life. The voice on the other end said: "You report to work Monday at police headquarters as a cadet."

If any strings were pulled for me—and I assumed they were—I never knew about them. All I knew was that I was ecstatic over the news. My mother, on the other hand, was less than thrilled.

"Why the city police?" she asked. "Why can't you work for one of the county departments?"

"Real police work in the city," I answered.

Was that youthful arrogance talking? Maybe to some degree. But I really believed it, too. When I thought of county cops, I thought of the beefy guys who chased after us on the golf course at night when they caught us drinking beer—and then took our beer when we fled!

The city was where the action was. That was where you went if you wanted a career chasing the bad guys. Not that my explanation made my mom feel any better.

That weekend, I went on a mini-shopping spree. I bought black shoes, a white shirt, a black tie and black pants, the spiffy, ultra-fashionable uniform of your basic police cadet. I showed up that first day nervous as hell and was assigned to the planning and research unit, where my tasks consisted of a) doing no planning and b) doing no research. Instead, I filed papers all day.

My jittery state of mind didn't exactly improve at lunch. That's when I bit into a hotdog at Pollack Johnny's and a stream of mustard splattered all over my new white shirt, which I attempted to conceal with the clever re-positioning of my tie.

I never found out if any of my new bosses were aware of

the mustard fiasco or the bumbling tie camouflage. But they wouldn't have been surprised by it. As we were told over and over again: there was nothing lower in the police department than a cadet.

Cadets, it was said, were even lower than Frankie the elevator operator, who, in terms of general intelligence, aptitude and initiative, was thought to be one of the lowest human beings on the planet.

But somehow I survived the ensuing months and in June of 1981, just before I turned 21, I went into the police academy. A little over four months later, I was a full-fledged cop, assigned to the Northeastern District.

I started on the midnight shift. On my first night, my partner was an old-timer named Harry Weimer. At 2:30 in the morning, we pulled into a Jewish cemetery off Moravia Road. Harry looked at me and said: "Rookie, you're in the backseat."

Thus was I introduced to the time-honored tradition of "going in the hole," where on-duty police officers find a nice secluded spot to nap in their patrol cars.

With seconds, my veteran partner was snoring contentedly. But there was no chance of me being able to sleep. Are you kidding? I was scared shitless. My head was on a swivel.

First of all, I'm in a cemetery in the dead of night, which was bad enough. Also, I don't want to get caught. Also, I don't want to get fired. Also, I don't want to get jumped by any psychos roaming around. And finally, I don't want any ghosts coming out of their tombs to haunt me for the rest of my life.

At this point, I should probably note that Harry did not simply take a quick cat nap that night. No, it was more like someone had whacked him over the head with a shovel. He was out for a good three-and-a-half hours before we resumed our patrol.

Harry Weimer turned out to be a great cop—and a great friend, too. I learned so much from him and so much from the other seasoned officers. I watched how they handled domestic-trouble calls, how they talked to drunks, how they conducted themselves during traffic stops.

That first night was the only time I rode with someone else. After that, I was on my own, riding around in a department-issued Ford sedan with a blue bubble light. Those cars didn't even have sirens—you beeped your horn a lot when gunning it through intersections during a car chase or responding to a call.

It didn't take long for the deadly serious nature of my new job to come into focus.

By the early 1980's, crack was becoming a big problem in Baltimore, as it was in many cities throughout the country. Violent Jamaican gangs had taken over the marijuana trade while the local knuckleheads, equally brutal, were warring over the cocaine and heroin markets.

The streets were awash in guns and there were plenty of bad actors willing to kill anyone perceived as a threat to their burgeoning drug empires.

A dangerous city was becoming ever more dangerous for its citizens—and for the brave men and women sworn to protect it.

Soon enough, a pair of high-profile cop-killings would serve as a sobering reminder of what everyone who wore the uniform faced every day.

3.

The War on Drugs Takes a Good Man

I was a young patrol officer in December of 1984 when the shooting death of Baltimore Police Detective Marcellus Ward was captured in a chilling audio recording that shook the department like few other incidents in its history.

"Marty" Ward, 36, was working undercover late that afternoon with a federal Drug Enforcement Administration task force in southwest Baltimore. In a third-floor apartment above a candy store, he had brokered a heroin buy from a man named Lascell Simmons, 26. The deal had just been captured on a live audio feed when members of the raid team rushed up the narrow staircase to make the arrest.

Apparently thinking rival dealers were coming for him, Simmons panicked. He pulled out a .357 Magnum and shot Ward four times as he sat on a couch. The gunfire and the soft moans of the dying cop could be heard on the recording. So could the harrowing cries of "Marty! Marty! Marty!" from his partner, Detective Gary Childs, standing on the stairs below.

Childs screamed for the shooter to throw down his weapon. This set off a tense exchange between the two that sounded like a Hollywood movie, but was instead all too real.

"I ain't throwing no gun down till the police come," Simmons replied, as quoted in a 1985 *Baltimore Sun* story. "Don't come up here, man. I'm telling you, wait until the police come, man. I can't let y'all up here because I don't know who y'all is."

"I *am* the f.... g police! Here's my badge!" Childs shouted, throwing the badge up to Simmons. "Now throw the gun down and walk down, and if that man dies, I'll kill you!"

As described in the dry vernacular of a police tribute page for Ward, "a brief period of negotiation" ensued. Then Simmons threw two handguns into the hallway and surrendered. By the time task force members entered Simmons' apartment, Marty Ward was dead.

As unsettling as that tape was when I heard it weeks later, what I also heard was the love Gary Childs had for his partner. I was amazed, too, at how focused he remained on doing whatever needed to be done to get to his friend.

While you could hear the fear and incredible anguish in his voice as he cried "Marty! Marty! Marty!" it was not the voice of panic.

Gary knew he and the others in the raid team were at a severe tactical disadvantage standing at the bottom of the stairs. By throwing his badge up to the bad guy, he probably prevented a major gun battle that surely would have ended up with more dead cops and DEA agents.

Still, it must have been awfully hard for Gary to disregard

all his training and experience and make the split-second decision to use his badge to defuse the situation so he might reach his mortally-wounded partner.

And then to burst into the apartment and find Marty already dead... my heart broke for Gary. I couldn't imagine the torment he went through.

How is this good man going to survive? I wondered in the days that followed. Because clearly, Gary was a victim. Not as much as Marty, a 13-year city police officer and a married father of two. But along with Marty's family, Gary was a victim nonetheless. And I wondered if he'd be irretrievably broken from the experience.

But he was not. Not by a long shot.

Instead, Gary Childs would go on to become a highly-decorated narcotics and homicide detective, one of the finest in the history of the Baltimore Police Department, in my view. And after the killing of Marty Ward, the department's policies regarding undercover drug buys would change dramatically.

The dangerous, time-consuming, manpower-intensive and meticulously-planned buys would now be used only to bring down the biggest dealers, the ones known to be supplying the largest quantities of the drugs that were poisoning the city.

My own thinking about the so-called "war on drugs" seemed to whip-saw back and forth, too. Was fighting it worth the cost? Would Marty Ward be just another dead cop in the futile attempt being waged to rid the streets of dope?

There was already talk of throwing in the towel and legalizing drugs. At first I thought: *Why not? Let the bastards kill themselves and each other, so long as my family and friends are safe.*

But I knew instinctively, like most rational folks, that legalization would not stop the killing of citizens and would actually lead to more death and destruction. With drugs even more accessible, more people would surely get hooked.

And no matter who was selling the drugs legally—whether it was the government or a private entity—there would always be an army of unsavory characters ready to step out of the shadows and whisper to potential buyers: "Hey, my stuff's cheaper. Better quality, too."

No, drug dealers wouldn't go away. Legalization sure as hell wouldn't make them think: *Guess I gotta go work at Target now.* There was way too much easy money—millions and millions of dollars—to be made.

And what message would legalization send to our children? That a life as an addict is a fine thing to aspire to? There were already kids in the city running the streets at all hours of the night because mom and dad were out selling dope to get high, or because the parents were already too zonked out to notice their kids were gone.

No, we needed to help these neighborhoods by getting as many dope dealers off the streets as possible. I had already started thinking about being a drug cop, and that maybe I could help the situation in these forlorn, drug-infested parts of the city in some small way.

Not only that, but I knew it would help me achieve my ultimate goal of one day joining the homicide unit, too.

To get to homicide, you had to make a name for yourself. The way to do that back then was to start in the various lower-level drug units, doing street buy/busts, rolling up on corners and chasing dealers and hiding in abandoned buildings to observe and record illicit transactions.

From there you'd move up to the CID (Criminal Investigation Division) Narcotics Section as a detective. This unit operated out of the downtown police headquarters building and worked on major cases throughout the city. There were also extensive overtime pay opportunities there.

Federal funds were coming in to help Baltimore pay its police to work extra hours and hopefully make a dent in the burgeoning heroin and crack cocaine markets. As a newly-married cop living in the city, I wanted nothing more than to start a family and live in the suburbs. Steady OT could definitely help with that.

From CID drugs, the next stop for an ambitious officer with smarts was homicide. Good drug cops, it was felt, made for great homicide detectives. And I wanted to be a great homicide detective.

I didn't want to ride a horse.

I didn't want to jump on a motorcycle.

I wanted to work in homicide.

Marty Ward's death had made me even more determined to land where I might help stop the wave of remorseless killings that had washed over the city for years.

4.

Vince Adolfo Was Me

If the killing of Marty Ward cast a pall over the BPD, the 1985 murder of Vincent Adolfo was even more disturbing to young officers like me who were patrolling the streets and still learning the ropes.

Vince, on the force only a few years, was in his marked patrol car on Nov. 18 when he spotted a late-model Cadillac in East Baltimore with a missing window covered with plastic.

A routine check of the license tags determined the car had been stolen in Queen Anne's County a month earlier. Adolfo radioed for back-up help, activated his blue emergency lights and followed the Cadillac and its four occupants.

When Adolfo and another officer attempted to box in the Cadillac with their cars, the driver bailed. He ran into an alley as his vehicle crashed into the second police cruiser.

While the officer in that car held the three other passengers at gunpoint, including one armed with a gun, Vince chased after the driver. This would turn out to be Flint Gregory Hunt, a career criminal with a propensity for violence who had spent years shuttling in and out of prisons.

After a brief foot-race, Adolfo caught Hunt and put him up against a wall. But when he attempted to handcuff him, Hunt resisted, holding onto a sign post. He managed to push Vince, causing him to lose his balance. Hunt then pulled a .357 Magnum Blackhawk from his waistband and shot Adolfo in the chest at close range, the bullet piercing the officer's armored vest and tearing through his right lung.

Reeling from his wound, Adolfo staggered away as Hunt cocked his gun and fired a second time. This time the high-caliber slug struck the young officer in the back and blew his heart apart. He collapsed in the back yard of a row house, his service weapon still resting in his lap.

Police officers and paramedics frantically performed CPR, but were unable to resuscitate Adolfo. He was taken to nearby Johns Hopkins Hospital, but died before a heart surgeon could operate on him. He was 25 years old.

Hunt fled the scene and a city-wide manhunt ensued, conducted by scores of uniformed and plainclothes officers as well as SWAT teams. Black-and-white mug shots of the suspect were shown everywhere.

At the Eastern District, grieving cops sobbed openly, bowed their heads and held a moment of silent prayer for their fallen colleague. They listened quietly as their leader, Lt. Tom Keavney, implored them not to let their desire for vengeance overwhelm them if they were fortunate enough to capture Hunt.

"Please," he said, according to a report in the *Sun*, "if you see the rotten bastard out there, do it by the book, OK?... Do it by the book."

The message was clear: no street justice.

"Vinnie was 100 percent man and 100 percent cop, and he died a very honorable death," Keavney had reminded his officers earlier. "Let us remember that we are honorable men and women, and that's what puts us above the stuff we have to deal with on the streets."

(On the other hand, the lieutenant could say whatever he wanted. Every cop in the room knew this: if that rotten bastard Hunt so much as flinched when he was caught, he'd never make it to court.)

I was just waking up from a nap prior to working the midnight shift that evening when a neighbor told me the news of Vince's death was all over the TV. Sitting on the front steps at my home in northeast Baltimore, I wondered if Vince had a wife and kids, and I said a prayer for this brave officer and his family.

Normally, I'd leave for work at 10:45, change at the District, play some pool and kibitz with the guys. But on this night, I went in at 9 and the mood was somber. We stayed glued to the TV, desperate for any info on Vince's killer. Everyone was chomping at the bit to hit the streets and look for this guy, whose name and description we now had.

There were lots of reasons why Vince Adolfo's death hit me and my fellow officers especially hard. This was a patrol guy, for one thing. This was a guy doing what we did every night, doing a dirty job to keep the city safe.

He'd been returning from a meal run, picking up food for the prisoners locked up in the Eastern District cellblock, when he spotted the stolen car. And like the conscientious and dedicated cop that he was, he immediately sprang into action.

He could have ignored the Caddy and finished delivering

the meals. This wasn't a service call. This was what we called "on view," meaning a police action Vince initiated. And it was the right thing to do, what we want all good cops to do. Besides, chasing car thieves and drug dealers was what most of us in patrol lived for.

There was another reason why I found his death so jarring. No, I had never met him. But hearing about him, I realized Vince Adolfo was *me*. I was a young cop, newly-married, still learning on the job, just as he was.

And his stop of the Cadillac was pretty much textbook. Upon learning it was stolen, he called for back-up and followed the car at a distance and asked if Foxtrot, the police helicopter, was available to assist. (It wasn't in the air at the time.) He did all the right things to stop a car thief and protect the citizens of Baltimore.

Police would soon discover that after shooting Adolfo, Hunt had called a friend and asked him to hide the murder weapon. He also told the friend that he had just shot a police officer, and wasn't sure if the cop was alive or dead.

Now, Flint Gregory Hunt was a desperate fugitive.

He was still on the loose when Vince Adolfo was laid to rest on Nov. 22, a cold and rainy day in the city. Some 800 people shoe-horned into Our Lady of Fatima Catholic Church for the funeral mass. Dignitaries on hand included the city's fiery mayor, William Donald Schaefer, City Council President Clarence Du Burns and Rep. Helen Delich Bentley, along with every other high-profile politician and civic leader who could squeeze in the aisles, hoping to be seen on the 6 o'clock news.

"My wish," the Rev. John O'Toole told the mourners, "is that your prayer will be for all who are here this afternoon, officers of the law and officials of our state . ... the guys and the gals who are on our side, that God will protect them so that we do not lose any more."

Even as Adolfo's casket, draped with the American flag, was borne through a police honor guard from the church to a waiting hearse for the trip to Oak Lawn Cemetery in Eastpoint, the search for Flint Gregory Hunt was intensifying.

Our detectives had determined he was no longer in town; the manhunt was now a multi-state affair. The 16-year-old Baltimore girl he had reportedly been traveling with was soon taken into custody in Philadelphia. Hunt himself had been spotted driving a stolen car in Camden, N.J., across the Delaware River from the City of Brotherly Love.

But "his whereabouts," a police spokesman told the media, "are completely unknown."

Finally, there came a break in the case: detectives learned Hunt had purchased a one-way bus ticket from Philadelphia to Santa Monica, California. He was said to be armed with two .357 Magnums. And two days after Vince Adolfo's coffin was lowered into the sodden ground of his final resting place, the man who killed him was arrested without incident at a Greyhound bus station in Tulsa, Okla.

As often happens in these cases, no small amount of luck was involved.

A middle-aged woman from New York City had been traveling on the same bus as Hunt. Just before police and FBI agents boarded the bus in Harrisburg, Pa., to flash photos of Hunt and alert passengers to be on the lookout for him, she had observed Hunt quietly disembark.

He had boarded the bus again after the law enforcement agents left. And after watching him fidgeting in his seat overnight and wondering if this was the man being sought, the woman had reported Hunt to a bus station employee, who called police.

The news of Hunt's arrest was widely celebrated back in Baltimore, especially at the Eastern District police station. Yet it was also a bittersweet moment for those still shocked and saddened by Vince Adolfo's murder.

"No matter what happens, it will not bring the man back," one officer told reporters. "There is a good young officer who is no longer with us."

Now it would be up to the courts to put Vince's killer away forever.

We prayed—again—that they would do just that.

5.

"God... Where Were You?"

If there's a portrait of searing grief that stands out among the many families of fallen police officers I've known, it may well be in the person of Karen Joy Adolfo, Vince Adolfo's widow.

The two were the very definition of childhood sweethearts. Karen Blank was 12 and Vince Adolfo 16 when they first met. Her parents had bought a summer home on Miller's Island, a sleepy enclave on a peninsula in southeastern Baltimore County that snakes into the Back River on one side and the Chesapeake Bay on the other. Vince worked summers there at a boatyard owned by the grandfather of his best friend, Ed Hann.

Karen wasn't allowed to date until she turned 16. But once she did—"I was very mature for my age"—she and Vince had eyes only for each other. Karen lived in Reisterstown and Vince lived in Eastpoint. But he would ride his bike the 30 miles to her house or take the bus, which often involved a ride of three hours or more.

From the beginning, Karen found Vince to be funny, considerate and ever-playful. On Christmas Eve of 1981, Vince picked her up and took her to his parents' house. The plan was for the two of them to attend Mass with his mother, Hilda Adolfo.

When talk turned to the traditional holiday picture-taking, Karen was surprised to find the family curiously absorbed with the train garden Vince had set up around the Christmas tree.

Someone said: "Put the train garden on, Karen!"

Karen was nonplussed. *Why do I have to do it?* she thought. *I don't even know how...*

But someone told her what switch to hit, and here came the little toy train flying around the track. She slowed it down and it came to a stop in front of her. On the back of one of the cars was a tiny box. Nestled inside was a gleaming diamond engagement ring.

"Is this for me?" Karen blurted.

But a look at Vince's smiling face and the flashes of photos being snapped left no doubt that it was. And on Sept. 24, 1983, she and Vince were married in the cozy chapel at Sacred Heart Church in Glyndon.

Vince was already a city police officer at that point. Originally, his dream was to build houses, and maybe one day start his own construction company. He had built their little starter home on Miller's Island, a labor of love that showed off his carpentry and handyman skills, as well as his penchant for hard work.

But when a drunk driver ran a red light and plowed into his motorcycle, Vince ended up in the hospital. His injuries were extensive, chief among them a broken collarbone and fractured ribs. Laid up, with mounting bills, he decided the vagaries of construction work wouldn't do for an ambitious young man with a fiancé and a desire to someday start a family.

It was time to put down his tool belt. He needed steady work.

When Vince spotted an ad for candidates interested in applying to the Baltimore police academy, he showed it to his friend Ed Hann. "They're hiring," Vince told him. The two took the entrance exam together.

Vince's family was dead set against him becoming a city cop. But Vince's mind was made up. He still loved building houses, creating something from nothing with his hands and his sweat and his drive and imagination. He thought he could still do that as a second job.

"But the stability, the health insurance, the fact he'd have a pension," convinced him that joining the police department was a solid career move, Karen recalled wistfully. "And he wanted to do good. He was proud to be a police officer.

"I remember he was very proud of the badge and proud to represent it," she continued. "He would always comment on how it was the best-looking badge around. Better than the country officers' badges and the state troopers' badges. It was bigger and shinier, he said."

Six weeks after joining the academy, Vince was patrolling the streets of the Eastern District. He took to the job naturally. He was a good, aggressive cop, especially well-suited, due to his natural athleticism, to chasing down the bad guys in foot races, which he did frequently and with relish.

Yet he had a sensitive side to him, too.

"He loved being a police officer," Karen said. "But he

would get discouraged at times."

The crushing poverty he saw in the city on a daily basis bothered him. So did the boundless drug addiction he encountered, the zombie parade of junkies and dealers shuffling listlessly on the streets of Baltimore from morning until night.

He hated the way some residents, either because of apathy, ignorance, stress or their own personal demons, used foul language around their children. He'd call them out on it, too. "Hey, your kids are here!" he'd remind them.

Sometimes the offender would appear chastened. At other times, Vince was more likely to earn a big "Fuck you!" for his trouble.

The pronounced wealth iniquity in the city bothered him, too.

"There was a Catholic girls school in the Eastern District, in a poor area," Karen recalled. "Vince was in his car, stationed there for when classes were dismissed for the day. And he saw this young boy in front of the school playing with little cars on the sidewalk."

For whatever reason, the sight of the boy playing with his modest toys when all these seemingly-more privileged girls spilled out of the school after the final bell bothered him, Karen recalled.

"So he'd give the kid money so he could go buy some candy," she said. "He enjoyed making connections with people. And being able to do kind-hearted things."

On another occasion, Vince caught a woman shoplifting food from a grocer. Feeling sorry for her, he paid the grocer for the items.

"He never told me about doing things like that," Karen said. "He never boasted about it. I would usually hear about it from other people."

On the November afternoon that Vince was killed, Karen had returned from her job at the NSA in Fort Meade, changed her clothes and gone off to a ceramics class in Dundalk with her two sisters-in-law.

The three women were in a back room talking about the upcoming holidays when Karen heard someone say: "Police officers are here." At first, Karen thought one might be Vince.

"Because in different places, never in uniform, he would just pop up," she explained years later. "So I thought: 'Oh my gosh, he's gonna get in trouble! What's he doing here?' I thought maybe he just came to say 'Hey, I'm in the area.'"

She heard a woman say: "Karen, can you come here? They're here to see you."

But it wasn't Vince standing there in the dim light. One of the officers was John Gilden, Vince's friend. Two other policemen accompanied him.

When she saw the ashen looks on their faces—and when Vince's brother Fred suddenly appeared—she knew something terrible had happened to her husband.

She remembers turning and trying to flee out the back door, to run away, to run anywhere she could, before the officers could say anything.

"It's OK, Karen," she heard Fred say. "Vince is in God's hands now."

In her frenzied state, with her mind racing, she took that to mean that Vince was going to be OK, that God was going to take care of him. It gave her hope.

"Because Vince had faith in God for his protection," Karen explained 36 years later, her voice breaking at the memory. "Because when I would worry about him, he always told me

'Don't worry, I have the best protection.' Meaning God. He always prayed to God to bring him home safe."

Now her only thought was to get to Vince's side as quickly as possible.

"Oh, my God, you gotta get me to him!"she cried out. "GET ME TO HIM! HE NEEDS ME!"

The harrowing trip to Johns Hopkins Hospital in the back of a police car was a jumble of lights and noise that seemed to take forever.

"Hurry, hurry!" she kept saying. "Can't we go faster?"

One of the officers said they couldn't. This was maddening to Karen. Impossible to comprehend. Why didn't they have the blue lights on! Or the siren wailing!

Once at the hospital, she remembered dashing in the front door and running into a long hallway, shouting: "WHERE IS HE? WHERE IS HE?"

"Come in this room first," a woman instructed. There were a few people in there, but none that Karen recognized. She assumed they were hospital staffers. But then her father Stanley Blank, her brother Dave Blank and her sister, Debbi Colby materialized. And now someone was saying: "Karen, you need to understand he's gone."

But she couldn't accept that. It was too overwhelming. Instead, she sank slowly to her knees, her body suddenly so leaden she wondered if she'd ever be able to rise again.

Someone on the hospital staff asked if she wanted to see Vince. But she said no. The prospect terrified her.

"I'll always regret" that decision, she told me. "Because I was scared. I didn't know what it would be like to not have him turn to me. When I entered a room, he would always turn and smile. I didn't know what it would be like, what the extent of his injuries were.

"I felt guilty because I shouldn't have been scared. And I regret not having that time with him. (But) I didn't know what to expect. I had never lost anybody. Never lost a grandparent, an aunt or an uncle. I had never been to a funeral, or a viewing.

"And part of it was, I (still) didn't want to accept it."

Instead, she lay crumpled on the floor, even as family members tried to coax her into a chair. The pain wouldn't allow her to breathe. She felt she needed to get as low as possible, to somehow sink into a place where the agony might ease.

That night, she was driven to her mother's house on Miller's Island. There, the two stayed up all night talking until finally, overcome with numbness and exhaustion, Karen fell asleep wrapped in her mother's arms.

Before the viewing days later at Connelly Funeral Home in Essex, Karen was again filled with trepidation.

Would she be able to handle the sight of Vince's lifeless body, this time while she was surrounded by scores of friends, police officers and strangers who had come to honor him? "I don't know if I can do this," she told her family.

Vince's sister-in-law, Shelby Adolfo, walked her to the viewing room doorway, where Karen got her first look at the open casket in which Vince lay. Yet this time all her fears vanished as she rushed forward to be with him.

And now she couldn't stop touching him, touching his face and arms and chest, laying her head on him, and telling him over and over how much she loved him. Now she didn't want to leave his side, even as family members gently tried to guide her to a seat so others could pay their respects.

At one point, a disheveled man in dirty clothes walked

into the room. The sight of him startled Karen and made her uncomfortable. Other officers demanded to know what the man was doing there, until someone recognized him as a homeless person from East Baltimore.

He explained that he had walked all the way to Essex to pay his respects to "Officer Vincie."

"He said Vince had once given him a pair of gloves to keep his hands warm," Karen recalled years later. "And I remembered those gloves—I had given them to Vince for Christmas one year.

"He never told me he had given them away. (But) I guess it was a cold night and someone needed them more than he did."

The weeks and months that followed were a blur of sorrow and pain and tears that seemed never-ending. Karen was inconsolable, cocooned 24 hours a day in her grief. Almost nothing in life seemed to matter anymore.

"Going to sleep was my (only) escape," she told me. "Because then I could be with Vince. I could close my eyes and fall asleep that way. The hard part was waking up in the morning. Every time I woke up… it was like reality. I was facing it (again.)"

She also found herself questioning God, as so many other grieving widows and widowers had done before her—since the beginning of time, really. Had her husband's unshakable faith in the boundless protection of the Creator been for naught? Wasn't that the spiritual life insurance policy he prayed for every time he slipped on his uniform and affixed his badge?

"I got very upset with God," Karen admitted. "Like: 'Where *were* you? He trusted you to be with him. Why weren't you with him to save him?'"

It would be years before the anguish and torment that were her constant companions began to lift—and only ever so slightly at first. Through a friend at work, she met a fellow NSA employee named Ron Vida who made her laugh again for the first time in ages. The two were married in 1998.

"I never had any intention of marrying again," she said. Losing someone the way she lost Vince, she went on, "is not like a divorce, where you stop loving someone. You're always loving that person."

She smiled wearily. "I read somewhere that it takes a special person to marry a widow."

The 1997 execution of Flint Gregory Hunt, her husband's killer, marked another milestone on the long road to recovery. Karen was sorry to see a man lose his life after her husband had lost his. But she saw the execution as justice, not vengeance

"That was closure," she said. "That felt good. I felt like it gave me peace."

A few days later, she heard an old song from the 1970's playing on the radio. It was "I Can See Clearly Now" by Johnny Nash, a feel-good number that reached no. 1 on the "Billboard Hot 100" charts back in the day.

"I heard those lyrics: 'It's gonna be a bright, bright, sunshiny day.'" Here she paused and smiled softly again. "And that's how I felt. Now I can have a life."

6.

"Why Are You Arresting My Son?"

In the summer of 1986, two events occurred that made me wonder—not for the first time—if I wanted to remain a police officer.

On a sweltering hot day, I was on patrol in sector 2 of the Northeast District, not exactly a hotbed of major crime—violent or otherwise. The area, racially diverse, mostly consisted of well-kept row homes and larger single-family houses occupied by a mix of working-class and middle-class families.

At an intersection near Coldspring Lane and Morgan State University, I spotted a suspicious-looking late-model sedan heading west. What attracted my attention was that the driver, a young African-American male, looked barely big enough to see over the steering wheel.

He gave me a quick, furtive glance and I ducked in behind him while checking out the "hot sheets" to see if the car was stolen. It was.

(Back then, police cars had no computers. The "hot sheets" were literally sheets of paper that were handed out every day at roll call containing the tag numbers of recently-stolen vehicles. These sheets were either taped or thumb-tacked to the dashboard, with the sticky adhesive residue and myriad pin holes left behind adding to the already shabby, run-down look of our cars.)

"I got one on the hot sheet," I radioed the dispatcher. I hit my lights and the sedan pulled over, almost careening into a bus stop.

As soon as it came to a stop, the driver bolted and took off running north across the empty college campus. I took off after him. The foot race was on. Except I was at a decided disadvantage: a 26-year-old cop in full uniform, wearing boots and weighed down with a duty belt that contained my service weapon, handcuffs and other tools of the trade, chasing a young skinny kid in a T-shirt, shorts and sneakers.

Did I mention how hot it was?

At this point, I should also reveal that my nickname growing up was "Turtle." On the other hand, I *did* run cross-country in high school, a sport that rewarded endurance more than speed. And endurance was what was surely needed now as we ran between the buildings at Morgan and the suspect began to pull away.

As I ran, I called in on my lapel radio, sending out a description of the kid and the direction in which we were headed. My goal was simply to keep him in sight until back-up arrived.

(A word or two about police radio transmissions. Sometimes, breathless and excited during a chase like this, cops get on the radio and, with a screechy and high-pitched voice, sound like they just hit puberty.

(Trust me: this is *not* what you want to sound like when you call in. Because your brothers and sisters in blue who hear it will wear you out with unceasing ridicule. Instead, you want to seem calm and collected, which of course you're not. Luckily for me, I've always had a deep, raspy voice which served me in good stead for moments like this.)

As we reached a long, empty campus parking area, the suspect began to play with me. He was so far ahead that he'd stop to catch his breath, then turn around and fix me with an amused smile before taking off again.

I kept yelling that I was going to kick his ass when I caught him. But looking back on it now, that threat might have been counter-productive. Hell, it probably motivated him to run even faster.

On and on we ran, me huffing and puffing and cursing, the kid loping effortlessly and more or less taunting me as he maintained a big lead. Then, in the distance, I heard the beautiful sound of sirens wailing. The cavalry was on its way!

Seconds later, another wonderful sound echoed throughout the concrete canyons: the whirring rotor blades of Foxtrot, the police helicopter. I couldn't see it, but it was somewhere up above us and close by.

Junior was back to walking at this point. But hearing the chopper, he began to run again.

Suddenly, like something out of a war movie, Foxtrot came zooming out of the sky. Nose down and tail up, it appeared to be skimming just a few feet above the ground and headed straight for the juvenile.

It was a fearsome sight. I had never seen anything like it.

Most of the Foxtrot pilots back then were highly-trained

ex-military guys, many having served in Vietnam during the war. That's all we hired at the time. They were fearless airborne cowboys with thousands of hours of flight time who thought nothing of hurtling around high-rises and swooping low over courtyards and alleyways to chase the bad guys.

It's safe to say these pilots were not wrapped too tight. And I mean that in the best possible way. Here they were in these tiny, claustrophobic Bell helicopters, essentially sealed in a glass bubble with an engine and tail rotor attached, performing all manner of daredevil stunts to help keep the citizens of Baltimore safe from criminals.

You had to love them. And all of us patrol guys did.

But back to the chase.

As Foxtrot barreled toward him, the young man finally had his come-to-Jesus moment. Quickly, he dropped to the asphalt in surrender. A few second later, I flopped on top of him, completely exhausted, not to mention rip-shit pissed.

"You're mine now!" I croaked. "As soon as I get you back in the wagon, I'm gonna kill you! You'll never go home again!"

Of course I had no intention of harming the kid. But I wanted him to pee his pants. I wanted him to soil himself. I wanted him to think: *I'm never gonna do this again.*

I placed him under arrest, put the cuffs on him and took him back to the Northeast District for processing. We needed to identify him, determine his age—he turned out to be 15— and whether he had a police record. (He didn't.)

Juvenile officers were summoned. They asked me to contact the boy's mother and see if he had a stable home to return to. I reached his sister and determined that he did. And after confirming a few other details, I put the boy in the back of my patrol car and took him home.

It turned out he lived in a nice neighborhood of row homes off Hillen Road. When we pulled up to the curb in front of his house, it seemed like the whole neighborhood was outside. There were children playing and adults chatting in small groups as I got the kid out of the car and walked him—still in handcuffs—up to the porch, where his mother was waiting.

If I expected her to be furious with her son, ashamed of his actions and embarrassed to see him being perp-walked in front of her neighbors, I was quickly disabused of that notion. Instead, the boy's mom tore into me.

"WHY ARE YOU ARRESTING MY SON?" she demanded in a loud and angry voice. "HE WAS ONLY GOING FOR A LITTLE RIDE! AND WHY IS HE IN HANDCUFFS?! HE'S ONLY A KID! AND WHY IS HIS SHIRT TORN?!"

I was stunned.

This was the complete opposite of what normally occurred when we brought juveniles home after an arrest. Many times, the parent accepting the wayward kid would start yelling at him and smacking him upside the head before we could even remove his handcuffs.

The discipline generally started right away. But not this time. Not only was she laying into me for doing my job, she was doing it right in front of her son! The instant message the boy received was this: *He didn't do anything wrong. He didn't need to be held accountable. It was the police who were the bad guys.*

It was not the first time I saw parents being less-than-sterling moms or dads. But the incident shocked me. It was so discouraging. It made me think: *Why are we, as police, doing this? Why did I just risk a heart attack and chase this kid halfway across the Northeast District in 90-degree-heat to make a good quality arrest?*

I realized then and there that some people just have no shot in hell of making it in this world. This poor kid had no chance with a mom like that. There was no doubt in my mind that he would not make it into adulthood without a serious criminal record. Which meant he had no chance at succeeding in life.

The incident shook me, and it caused me to again re-evaluate whether I wanted to remain a cop.

At the time, I was at the five-year mark in my career. Typically, that was a milestone that prompted many young officers to consider whether they loved the job enough to continue on the force, or whether it was time to try another career—one that hopefully paid better and was far less dangerous.

One where you didn't have to chase a 15-year-old kid on a broiling summer's day and wonder whether he'd whip out a gun and shoot you when you caught him.

The other thing driving my soul-searching was this: my wife Sandy and I had just found out she was pregnant with our first child.

We were elated at the news. But it begged the question: what kind of dad did I want to be?

I knew part of the answer. I wanted to go to ballgames with this child. I wanted to coach his or her Little League team. I wanted to be an active parent. But would the job of police officer allow me to do that?

If I stayed in patrol, it would. In patrol, you knew your schedule a full year in advance. You knew when you were working days, you knew when you were working nights. You knew your days off for the entire year.

But my goal had been to get to narcotics—and from there to land in my dream job in homicide. But narcotics was night work! Narcotics was weekends! It was not being home when so many sports and school activities normally take place.

As cliché as it sounds, my life was at a crossroads. Which path would I take?

Right now, the answer was clear as mud.

7.

Street Rips and Hounds From Hell

After months of agonizing, something happened that finally put my career indecision to rest.

For some time, I had made it known that I wanted to work in the Drug Enforcement Unit. So when the opportunity arose early in 1988 to "go upstairs" as we called it—to the second floor in the Northeast District, the unit offices—I jumped at it.

I was 28 and ecstatic to be selected, seeing it as confirmation that the higher-ups in the chain of command recognized my potential to do more expansive police work. The job entailed relatively low-to- mid-level narcotics and vice operations within the district. Yet it was still a stepping-stone to homicide. And now I was fully committed to what I hoped would be a long career with the department.

Understand, I still wanted to be an engaged parent. Our son Patrick was less than a year old and needed his dad to be around. Yet happily, the new job came with a more flexible schedule than I had originally envisioned. It also seemed to me that having a husband and father who *liked* going to work every day, who was *engaged* in his job instead of bitching and moaning about it constantly, would help the cause of family harmony.

Working in DEU, I learned that so much of the job was about building relationships with the people you worked with.

It wasn't necessarily about how good a cop you were, although that was important. But your bosses also needed to know they could trust you, that they didn't have to write up a lot of paperwork to explain any crazy decisions you made out on the streets, where there was already plenty of craziness.

In the DEU we'd do what were called "street rips." That is, we'd watch somebody purchase drugs from a covert location, such as an abandoned house or a parked car, and arrest them.

Or we'd do what were called "door pops." We'd roll up in our unmarked car to a known drug corner where a group of Baltimore's finest entrepreneurs were milling about, pop the door and chase after whoever ran.

The other part of the job entailed working street-level informants and having them buy drugs out of a house so we could then obtain search warrants and raid the place. The city was saturated with narcotics and my squad of five or six officers would do as many as 15-20 search warrants a month.

We served our own search warrants, too. Rarely were we accompanied by our Quick Response Team (our version of SWAT), unless it was thought the target was so heavily-armed that we'd be out-gunned. Instead, tense and adrenalized, we kicked down a lot of doors, never knowing what awaited us inside after shouting "POLICE! POLICE!"

The fact was, we worked off neighborhood complaints. The city at that time had a drug hotline called 685-DRUG. It was a great program. People could leave anonymous complaints about drug houses in their community. We'd get those complaints every day and prioritize them, determine which crack house—crack was mostly the drug of choice back then—we were going to hit.

The potential for something to go horribly wrong on these raids was ever-present. Looking back, our tactics were poor and we were simply lucky not to have someone shot or killed. Which was almost what happened one evening when we hit a two-story row house in the Four-by-Four, a small neighborhood in northeast Baltimore named for its four north-to-south streets and four east-to-west streets.

Often, we used sledgehammers and mauls to break down doors to get inside. But on this night, a guy in our unit, Perry Stanfield, was wielding the newest creative weapon in forcible entry: a steel pipe filled with concrete, with handles conveniently affixed to the top so it could be swung like a battering ram.

Perry was a huge man, maybe 6-foot-5 and 240 pounds, and strong as an ox. With Perry hammering a door, it was never a question of whether we'd gain access on the first blow. The question was how far the lock would shoot across the room once the door swung open. We actually kept a tape-measure and tracked his stats on these raids.

There were six of us on this one, plus a sergeant, a uniformed officer and someone outside watching the back door. (The uniformed cop was there so the people inside would realize it was the police hitting them, not rival dealers bent on robbery. Above all, we didn't want another mistaken-identity fiasco like the one that got Marty Ward killed.)

Bursting in with guns drawn, we saw two guys take off.

Everyone had an assigned area to cover on these raids. Mine was the first floor. When I saw a member of our unit, Dave Reitz, grab one of the occupants in the dining room and throw him up against the wall, I headed down to the basement, thinking Dave had the situation in hand.

Basements were always problematic. You were totally exposed, walking down a narrow flight of stairs. Generally, it was dark, which meant you were carrying a flashlight in one hand. And of course, with cops in boots thudding down creaking stairs, the bad guys could hear you coming.

Suddenly, as I started down, I heard a struggle behind me. Turning around, I saw Dave and the guy he'd tackled engaged in an all-out, no-holds-barred fight for Dave's gun. I ran back up and just as I was about to smash the guy over the head with my flashlight, Dave wrestled the gun away. Finally we got the guy on the ground and cuffed him.

Dave stayed with his guy, and now Perry and I and Craig Singletary, another member of our unit, continued downstairs. The brawl with the gun-grabber had been unnerving, mostly because I never should have left Dave until his guy was secure.

Now we were even more jangled, because that melee had delayed our rush to the basement, giving whoever was down there even more time to possibly grab a weapon and open fire when we reached the ground floor.

But there would be no more drama down there on this day. Instead, we found two men hiding under a bed, which is probably the worst place in the world to hide. Hell, dating back to your days as a kid playing hide-and-go-seek, didn't *everybody* look under the bed first?

Thankfully, neither man was armed and both surrendered peacefully. We later found two weapons in the house. But the truth was, the entire nerve-frying ordeal turned up no more than an ounce of crack cocaine.

The two clowns under the bed were the subjects of much joking when we all met later that night at a bar called the Cameo for some much-needed stress relief. Cops go to bars after work with their fellow cops not only for the alcohol, but to talk about how their day went—what went right, what went wrong—and to decompress before heading home.

Think about it: an hour earlier, you were busting down the door of a known drug house and getting in a do-or-die scrap with a cursing, wild-eyed stranger frantically clawing for your gun and looking to shoot you. And now you're going to head straight home and kiss the kiddies good-night in their cribs and try for some sense of normalcy?

Good luck with that plan.

The fact is, little is normal in a cop's life. That's why your friends tend to be fellow cops, especially when you work in a specialized unit like the DEU. You're working with these people day after day in high-stress situations, you're socializing with them, your family members are socializing with their family members.

You tend to be insular in terms of who you hang out with. You lose a lot of old friends when you become a police officer. A lot of your high-school buddies don't want to be around you anymore.

Maybe they're smoking weed or doing other drugs, or maybe they're involved in something else that tip-toes the lines of moral, ethical or criminal misbehavior. Whatever it is, you realize that suddenly you're not getting invited to the ballgames and the pool parties and the Christmas get-togeth-ers the way you once did. Thus you tend to rely more and more on the comradeship of your brothers and sisters in blue.

If the prospect of facing a whacked-out and desperate dealer with a gun was the no. 1 concern during our drug raids, no. 2 was probably dogs. Dogs—in particular the pit bulls and Rottweilers dealers used to protect their supply from the police and other dealers—were a huge problem.

Drug dealers would actually pull the claws of these ani-mals so we couldn't hear them coming at us. And, boy, would they come at us! A lot of cops were bitten by these dogs. Most times we had nothing to deal with the situation safely. The result, as ugly as it sounds, was that we shot a lot of dogs.

Finally our sergeant came up with an ingenious tool that helped greatly. He stuffed a latex glove on the end of an axe handle and wrapped it in duct tape. So when the dog charged, he'd feed it the axe handle. As the animal attacked that, we'd spray it with a fire extinguisher, which would disorient it long enough to use a dog pole.

This was a long metal pole with a noose on the end. If you got the noose around the dog's neck, you pulled tightly and that helped control the dog. But using the noose to hold off an enraged Rottweiler wasn't exactly like leisurely attempting to lasso a calf.

If you didn't have time to use a dog pole... well, as I said, we shot a lot of dogs.

At another evening drug raid in the Four-by-Four, we were leaving the back door of the house to inspect the garage, where an informant had told us crack or cocaine was stashed. Suddenly this damned Rottweiler came dashing around the corner, teeth out and snarling, ready to tear us up.

The jaws of these dogs were so powerful that if one got hold of a person's limb, it could snap a bone in a heartbeat. But there would be no bone-snapping this evening. As soon as the dog lunged, one of our unit, fearing the worst, shot it.

Now we were bummed. Not because the dog was dead; the beast would have surely attacked us and ripped one of us to shreds. No, we were bummed because now we'd have to write a report on the dog's death and the circumstances that led up to it.

This would involve a ton of time and paperwork. We would also need to include photos of the dead animal in any account of the incident.

On further inspection of the "crime scene," however, we came upon this startling realization: the dog had actually been tied up. Yes, it had looked like the proverbial hound from hell: a 130-pound ball of tightly-coiled sinew and muscle, rheumy yellow eyes radiating fury, fangs bared, spittle flying everywhere as it snapped and growled and prepared to launch itself at us.

Except… unbeknown to us, it had been secured by a thick, sturdy chain.

Which meant it never *could* have gotten to us.

Well. Now what to do? We huddled and came up with a plan.

Clearly, there was no getting out of filing a report on the tragedy. But in the photos of the deceased dog taken that day by our law enforcement heroes, the animal's chain was— ta-daa!—conveniently missing. Thus ended yet another saga of a police-dog encounter that could have gone terribly wrong but didn't—except, of course, for the dog.

Certainly it ended better than another infamous case in

the Southeast District, where a sergeant—we'll call him Bill Jones for the purposes of this story—was attacked during a drug raid by a Rottweiler and savagely bitten right below the belly button.

As frightening as that sounds, the encounter soon took on comical proportions, tapping the vein of dark humor that is practically baked into a cop's DNA.

As his partners tried frantically to pry the dog off him, the terrified Sgt. Jones drew his weapon and shot the animal. Unfortunately, the bullet went through the Rottweiler and tore into the sergeant's foot.

Yet as the poor man, bloodied and yelping in pain, was loaded into an ambulance for the trip to the ER, he seemed far more concerned about where the dog had bitten him than the slug he'd taken.

Nearing hysteria, he kept screaming to his partners: "IS MY JUNK STILL THERE?" Engulfed in laughter, they assured him they had absolutely no intention of checking his genitalia to see what was—or wasn't—still attached.

"Bill," they replied, not at all sympathetically, "they'll let you know at the hospital!"

God, no wonder I loved that job!

8.

Bust Five Johns and It's Miller Time

When those of us in the DEU weren't raiding drug dens and fending off frenzied killer dogs, we did vice work.

During the late 80's, there was a huge concentration of hookers and johns in the area of Pulaski Highway and Northpoint Road in East Baltimore. Cheap motels like the Drake, the Marylander and the New Motel proliferated, and prostitutes from all over the country worked the dreary swath of bars, strip clubs and truck stops near the Baltimore County line.

Prostitution is often called a victim-less crime, but if you see it close-up, day after day, you might not think so. Almost all the women were drug addicts: crack-heads or heroin users. At least a quarter of the hookers were transvestites.

Many had a history of being sexually abused. Many also had children of their own they were supporting.

"Our officers have arrested one woman who was a grand-mother, one seven months pregnant, and two sisters and their mother," a county police captain told the Sun. "During an eight-month period, we arrested 58 prostitutes, but how do you continue to do that with the jails packed with major violators?"

Where the hookers go, the pimps and drug dealers go, and violence from shootings, stabbings and all manner of other assaults invariably follows. Back then, the AIDS epidemic that began in the early 80's was intensifying, and HIV infections in the sex trade were rampant, too.

The johns were taking all manner of STDs home to their loved ones, raising alarms in the medical community.

The legitimate business owners along Pulaski Highway were up in arms, too, as street-walkers brazenly solicited their customers and shot dope in their parking lots. Many also wandered high as a kite into traffic, causing the screeching of tires, fender-benders and angry motorists spewing profanities at all hours.

It was an altogether depressing scene and our unit was in the thick of it on those nights when we were called to make arrests and alleviate the problem, which was like trying to beat back the tide.

It was always a quota game, this sort of work. The unit sergeant would give you the number of hookers or johns the squad was expected to arrest that evening. And as soon as you got your number—BINGO!—you were done for the night. Which invariably meant we'd happily spend the rest of the shift drinking at a bar somewhere.

(In the DEU, we always knew what we needed to do to look productive in the eyes of the command staff. You always wanted to beat last month's tally of arrests, but not by too much, lest next month's quota be set impossibly high.)

Yet even here, amid so much misery, we found a need to joke with each other and lighten the mood—if for no other reason than to preserve our sanity.

One night, it was decided we were going to arrest johns. The sergeant had given us our number: five. Bust five johns and it was Miller Time.

Piece of cake, we thought.

The Marylander at 6401 Pulaski Highway was our operational venue of choice, where the manager had given us a room and a key. Charmaine Thomas, an attractive woman in our unit, was the bait. A native of Allentown, Pa., who attended Loyola College in Baltimore, she was in her late 20's and took crap from no one.

The plan was for Charmaine to arrange the deal with the john out on the street. Then when the two would come to the room, ostensibly to consummate the sex act, she would open the bathroom door, where the rest of the unit was hiding.

This was the signal for us to pop out, handcuff the poor mope and have him stand—quietly—in the bathtub until our next, ahem, guest arrived.

When we reached our quota, we'd call for the transport wagon to take all five prisoners to jail. Then we'd call it a night and head off to the bar.

Around 7 o'clock, Charmaine went to work, strolling up and down in front of the hotel parking lot. Quickly, she reeled in her first john, a rec league soccer coach with a bag full of balls in the back of his car.

We didn't know if he intended to head to practice after his little assignation or not. But if he *did*, someone else was going to have run the practice, as the coach would be indisposed until after he was booked and saw a court commissioner.

Back on the street, Charmaine attracted the second john in no time. And the third one. And the fourth. As fast as we could search them, cuff them and stick them in the bathtub—warning them, in our usual polite way, to shut the fuck up—she hooked another.

Finally, maybe an hour after first hitting the street, she brought up the fifth john. Through a crack in the bathroom door, we could see it was an old guy in his mid-70's wearing a classic wife-beater T-shirt. He started unzipping his pants the minute he entered the room.

We were jubilant. *Quitting time was just around the corner!* Which meant it was the perfect time to have a little fun with our intrepid female colleague.

This time when she tried to signal us by opening the bathroom door, I held the doorknob tightly from the inside.

She tried opening it again. I held it even tighter. This tug of war, like something out of a Marx Brothers movie, went on for another 30 seconds. Charmaine, no fool, knew exactly what was going on. She could hear us cracking up.

"Get your fucking asses out here!" she hissed.

The geezer john, on the other hand, had no idea what was happening. He was in his own little world. By this point, he was almost buck-naked, too, and ready for some action.

Finally, we could contain ourselves no longer. We threw open the door to confront the frowning visage of our furious colleague, who looked like she would personally gut each of us with a rusty fishing knife if given the chance.

As for the old guy, even when we yelled "POLICE! POLICE!" and he spotted the badges hanging from our necks, he still seemed oblivious. Only after we handcuffed him and marched out the other four grim-faced knuckleheads, and sat them on the bed, did it seem to dawn on him that the party—well, *his* party anyway—was over.

Thankfully, Charmaine was a good sport. And by the time we all met at the bar later, she was no longer rip-shit pissed and able to laugh at the little stunt we'd pulled. Which was no surprise—if you couldn't take a joke, you were definitely in the wrong unit, and probably the wrong profession, too.

Another part of our work in vice involved policing the thousands of video poker machines installed in bars and restaurants all over the city. The use of these machines by patrons for "amusement purposes" was perfectly legal. What was *not* legal were the under-the-table payouts the owners of these establishments would invariably make to the winners of the games.

To combat this problem, we sent undercover cops into these places to hang out and develop relationships with the bar maids and bartenders, all the while watching to see if the poker players got paid.

As you can imagine, this sort of duty wasn't exactly like breaking rocks in the hot sun. Basically, you were sitting there in a cozy pub or eatery chatting with folks or watching TV and drinking on the city's dime.

I wasn't a big drinker, basically a two-beer guy, so I always hoped to make my observations without having to stay and guzzle for too long. One thing you *definitely* couldn't do is sit there without drinking.

In most of these little neighborhood dives, everybody knew the regulars. Someone would walk through the door and invariably be greeted like Norm Peterson—"*NORM!*"—on the old sitcom "Cheers." Folks could be suspicious of strangers.

So a newcomer suddenly spending a lot of time there without drinking would definitely have been regarded as a weirdo—or worse.

Once we spotted money changing hands after a win on the machines, we'd come back a few days later with a search warrant. The place would be shut down while we did the search, which usually took a few hours. Usually, we'd just issue a summons, unless we found drugs or something even more serious, like illegal weapons.

The liquor board would then get our report and take action. This usually resulted in a fine, or a short suspension of the bar's liquor license if this was a second or third violation.

The amount of money generated by those machines was huge, too. This was a whole underground economy. There were vending companies that sold those machines or rented them to bars in exchange for loans.

So if someone needed money to open a bar—say, $40,000 or $50,000—it wasn't uncommon for one of these vending companies to say: "We'll give you the machines and we get a big slice of the profits."

Or even *all* of the profits. And that's how the loan would be paid back.

Still, there were city fathers and local clergy and politicians thundering about the "moral turpitude" caused by these poker machines. Ordinary citizens were concerned about loved ones with gambling addictions falling prey to them, too.

Wives would call us with horror stories about husbands losing their paychecks playing the machines, and they'd rat out the specific bar where the poor dope lost it. And make no mistake about it, *all* these bars paid off on these machines. If they didn't, no one would bother to play them.

Originally, when an establishment got in trouble for pay-offs, we would seize the machines. We'd take them out on a dolly and put them in the back of a U-Haul and take them back to the district.

But that got to be crazy. It became too time-consuming to do all that, plus there was not enough storage space in the evidence room for all these big, clunky machines. Finally the courts started letting us take out the circuit boards, which would disable the machines and still leave us with evidence to prosecute cases.

But the machines wouldn't be out of commission for long. The bar owners would have to go to court, the liquor board would get involved, the owners would get fined—and the machines would end up right back in the same place, casting their mesmerizing spell on boozed-up patrons and generating thousands of dollars for the saloons.

I always had mixed feelings when we went back to bust a place for paying out on the machines. Here I had hung out there, sometimes for weeks, eating and drinking, laughing and commiserating, befriending the people who worked there and being befriended in turn.

And now I had returned to get them in trouble and hurt their livelihood. They thought it was a pretty shitty thing to do. I couldn't blame them for thinking that way, especially the owners of these little neighborhood joints that were just getting by.

It sucked sometimes. It really did.

But this was my job. I had taken an oath to uphold the laws of the city and the state—no matter how shitty it made me feel at times.

9.

The Embodiment of Hannibal Lector

In the late summer of 1990, the citizens of Maryland were alternately horrified and riveted by the murderous crime spree of a man named John Frederick Thanos. Due in no small part to the savagery of his actions, and his seeming indifference to the suffering he caused, it was also the case that helped solidify my feelings about the death penalty.

Thanos was a career criminal who had already spent most of his 41 years behind bars for a laundry list of charges, including rape and armed robbery. Yet this seemed like a mere prelude to the tragic events that unfolded, first on the Eastern Shore and later in the Baltimore suburbs, as Labor Day weekend approached.

Mistakenly let out of prison 18 months early after doing time on the robbery charge, Thanos had found work as a chicken processor on the night shift at a Perdue plant in

Salisbury. But on Friday, August 29, he cashed his paycheck, bought a .22-caliber rifle and sawed off the barrel so it would fit in a leather doctor's bag.

He used his new toy that night to rob a Salisbury cab driver and force him into the trunk of his car. When the cabbie protested, Thanos became impatient and barked: "If you don't stop all this nonsense, I'm going to blow you away."

Thanos drove around in the cab for hours until finally abandoning it. The next day, he was hitch-hiking on Route 50 when 18-year-old Gregory Taylor, a high school student and welder, stopped to give him a ride.

Thanos pulled out the rifle and ordered Taylor to drive to a remote area, where he planned to tie him to a tree and flee with the car. But when the terrified Taylor balked at being bound and begged for his life, Thanos, according to his confession, shot him.

Asked by the cops why he killed Taylor, Thanos shrugged and said: "He was a constant nuisance. Whining. He didn't want to cooperate. So I got fed up and just shot him in the head.

"I took him, found a place, laid him down," Thanos continued. "He still didn't want to be tied up, so I shot him in the head three times, and I left."

Less than 24 hours later, Thanos tried to rob a convenience store in Salisbury. When things went awry, he shot the clerk in the head. Luckily, the bullet only grazed the man's scalp, at which point Thanos panicked and took off.

Traveling west in Gregory Taylor's car, he stopped to dye his hair black to look more like Taylor, apparently convincing himself the 23-year age difference between the two would go unnoticed.

Arriving in Middle River outside Baltimore, he stopped at a gas station where a 16-year-old named Billy Winebrenner was working. Thanos told the boy he had no money. Instead, he proposed trading his father's gold watch—a retirement gift the younger Thanos had somehow acquired—for $20 and gas.

There were strings attached to the deal, however: Thanos explained he wanted to come back, pay the teenager $60 and get the watch back.

When Thanos returned two days later, Billy was at the gas station with his 14-year-old girlfriend, Melody Pistorio. The boy explained he didn't have the watch and told Thanos it was in a jewelry box at Melody's house.

Apparently enraged, Thanos pulled the rifle from his doctor's bag and instructed the two teenagers to fill the bag with cash. Even though they cooperated and were, in his words, "perfectly good" throughout the ordeal, he shot each twice in the head.

The bloody rampage might have continued when Thanos returned to Salisbury. Except this time his car was spotted by police, who recognized it as matching the description of the vehicle seen leaving the convenience store robbery days earlier.

A wild car chase ensued into Delaware. There, Thanos eluded the cops and other law enforcement agencies, abandoned the car, carjacked another one and forced the driver at gunpoint to drive to a fast-food restaurant in Smyrna.

When police picked up his trail again and flooded into the parking lot, the desperate Thanos engaged them in a chaotic gun battle. Not until he was out of ammunition was he finally captured.

"I want to kill in order to be killed," his mother, Patti Thanos, quoted him as saying in an interview she did with *The*

Dispatch newspaper in Ocean City, Md. after his arrest. "He said he was getting too old and didn't have the guts to kill himself, so he was going to have a shootout with police."

During the numerous extradition hearings and court proceedings that followed, Thanos, despite his unimposing stature, cut a monstrous figure. Glowering and seemingly without remorse, he was by turns arrogant, threatening, sarcastic, profane and pontificating.

During one appearance, he said he wanted to dig up the bones of the young people he'd killed so he could "beat them into a powder and urinate on them and stir it into a murky, yellowish elixir and serve it up to those loved ones."

Little wonder that Thanos quickly became the poster boy for death penalty advocates. This was an empty husk of a man, a cold-eyed killer who repeatedly announced he wanted nothing more than to take another life if given the opportunity.

"You have nothing at all that's redeeming," said Sandra A. O'Connor, the Baltimore County state's attorney at the time, echoing the thoughts of so many. Then addressing the court, she added: "In my 26 years of prosecuting in Baltimore and Baltimore County, I don't know if I can think of a greater threat to society than him, if he were to escape."

In 1992, Thanos was convicted and sentenced to death for the killings of Greg Taylor, Billy Winebrenner and Melody Pistorio. At his sentencing hearing for the murders of the two youngsters at the gas station, during which Thanos might have been expected to plead for mercy, he spat: "If I could bring those brats back right now from their graves, I would do it so that I could murder them again before their eyes, as they cringe in fear and horror, reliving this eternal nightmare."

Here for all to see was the embodiment of another brutal

and infamous—if fictional—psychopath, Hannibal Lector. ("The Silence of the Lambs," the thriller starring Anthony Hopkins and Jodie Foster that made Hannibal the Cannibal a household name, had landed in movie theaters a year earlier.)

It was clear from the outset that Thanos wanted to die. He refused to appeal his death sentences and became angry when his mother and sister, his lawyers and the ACLU, filed appeals on his behalf.

I had followed the case closely, and I wanted him to die, too.

Like most cops I know, I strongly support the death penalty. Maybe because like most cops, I've seen up close and personal how some human beings are capable of the most violent, sickening and horrendous acts imaginable.

My take on the "ultimate punishment" is not simply a knee-jerk reaction of yet another Republican in law enforcement.

I don't believe every murder case should be a death penalty case. Our system of justice could not withstand the weight of having to prosecute dozens of cases in Baltimore City alone every year, cases with aggravating circumstances such as robbery, rape or the killing of a police officer among the yearly 300-plus homicides.

Capital punishment is currently authorized in 27 states. (Maryland is not one of them; then-Governor Martin O'Malley signed a bill outlawing it in 2013. Interestingly, O'Malley's position on the death penalty changed once he was elected governor.

(Earlier, while seeking the endorsement of the Fraternal Order of Police, he'd stated that he supported the death penalty. Yes, I know that's shocking: a politician changing his position on an issue after being elected.)

I don't believe the death penalty serves as a deterrent to crime in general in the 27 states that have legalized it, either. Or that it deters any person intent on committing murder, although there's no denying the ultimate punishment of death does prevent the convicted killer from killing again.

I simply believe that some murderers deserve to die for their heinous crimes, and that our society should not task law-abiding taxpayers and over-worked correctional officers with the burden of keeping a vicious killer alive.

Why should society wait for old age or disease to render the justice these killers deserve? And let's face it: the reason many death penalty opponents suggest life without parole as a more "just" sentence is simply because they hope one day the killer in question will be let out of jail due to changes in the law, or because a judge or a court somewhere tinkers with the sentence.

What also gets lost in the conversation are the victims. I'm not talking about the poor person who was raped and had her throat slit, or the corner grocery store clerk who was robbed and shot over $100 in the cash register.

I'm talking about the survivors directly impacted by the murder, too. The parents who had to bury a child. The husband or wife who lost a spouse and had to explain to a child that mommy or daddy would not be coming home because of the horrifying deeds of a "bad guy."

Those are the people who have to find a way to move forward, to find the will to live with the ghastly memories of how their loved ones were taken from this earth. The criminal justice system is supposed to serve them as well.

I understand, and even respect, many who do not believe in the death penalty—for example, someone who opposes it for religious reasons. But I draw the line with those who use false and misleading information to justify their opposition.

A favorite nugget of misinformation advanced by death penalty opponents is that innocent persons have been put to death by the state. But since the U.S. Supreme Court reinstated the death penalty in 1976, I have not been able to find a single case in which the court has declared a person innocent after being put to death.

According to the Death Penalty Information Center, a non-profit organization based in Washington, D.C., Maryland has had just one person whose death penalty sentence was overturned due to being proven innocent.

The other red herring put forth by the civil rights activist Jesse Jackson and others is that African-Americans are disproportionately put to death for capital crimes compared to white people.

The available statistics prove this to be false. Again, according to the Death Penalty Information Center, a group that is clearly anti-death penalty, while 13 percent of the U.S. population is African-American, roughly 41 percent of Death Row inmates are black. Yet such simple statistics of over-representation fail to prove racial bias.

The relevant population for comparison is not the general population but rather then population of murderers. The United States Department of Justice (DOJ) found that while African Americans constituted 48 percent of adults charged with homicide, they were only 41 percent of those admitted to prison under a death sentence.

In other words, once arrested for murder, African-Americans are actually less likely to receive a capital sentence than are whites.

Yet in the case of John Thanos, both those arguments, thankfully, did not come into play.

Thanos admitted to the murders and *asked* to be put to death. His testimony left no doubt that given the opportunity to kill again, he would—gleefully, even—whether back on the streets or behind bars.

And Thanos was white, as were all three of his victims1994, eliminating the issue of race altogether. His defense team would point to an abusive childhood (there was conflicting testimony on this) and argue that Thanos' bizarre rantings in court proved he was mentally incompetent.

Yet in the end, for prosecutors pushing for the death penalty, this case was a slam dunk.

Thus it was that early on the morning of May 17, 1994, Thanos became the first person in Maryland to be executed by lethal injection instead of the gas chamber—and the first to be put to death by the state since 1962.

Asked if he had any last words, Thanos responded: "Adios."

To which I replied: "Good riddance."

10.

Advocating For Cop Families in Crisis

By the early 1990's, after 10 years as a cop, there were aspects about the job that concerned me. In conversations with my dad, I was always bringing up command issues, the leadership short-comings I saw in the highest ranks of the police department.

For one thing, there was no attention being paid to officer wellness, specifically mental health. You were just expected to go out there and be a robot and do a job. Officers on the street would respond to the most horrific acts of violence and degra-dation—stabbings, shootings, gruesome car accidents, sexual assaults involving children—and end up trying to drink away what they'd witnessed, instead of getting the counseling and treatment they needed.

Command seemed indifferent to the incredible psycholog-ical toll these incidents could take. This was driven home to me one day when we received a call about a possible drowning at an apartment complex in the Northeast District.

We were told two young children had gone to the complex's swimming pool, which had not yet opened for the summer, to play with the German Shepherd watchdog there. When we got to the pool, the poor dog was frantically treading water in the eight feet of murky rainwater that had collected in the deep end. But there was no sign of the kids.

The rest of the pool was empty, but covered in a thick, green slime. It was so slippery we all lost our footing trying to retrieve the dog and assess the situation. When the fire department arrived, a firefighter with a rope tied around him waded into the deep end. But the water was so choked with mud and leaves and debris that he couldn't see a thing.

Finally the firefighters began using a dragging hook to probe the water. And within minutes the grim search yielded the lifeless body of a 10-year-old boy. We immediately began CPR on him; after the first breath I administered, he tossed up a huge stream of dirty green water that covered my face and uniform.

The body of the second child, an 11-year-old girl, was soon recovered. Efforts were made to revive her too. Both children were rushed to area hospitals, but it was clear both were already dead. Within minutes, the media began arriving. So did members of our command staff.

I remember sitting in a daze on a curb, with my shirt unbuttoned and my uniform splattered from head to foot with gunk and algae and what smelled like sewer water. A commander who shall remain nameless walked over to me.

I thought he'd ask a question or two about what had just happened, or maybe ask how I was doing after the ordeal. Instead, all he said to me was: "Officer, put your hat on."

That's how it could be on the job sometimes. And those hard-ass commanders who didn't have the decency to ask about their officers after a tragedy like this? We lost all respect for them.

Aside from the lack of support given to us city cops, there was also the matter of our pay and benefits, which were laughably lower than our counterparts in Baltimore County and the Maryland State Police. It was really a slap in the face, because we were doing twice the work, if not more, of the guys and gals who worked for those agencies.

We city cops used to say: "Five years on the streets of Baltimore, you'll see more and do more than a 25-year cop in Baltimore County." Which dove-tailed nicely with my own personal motto, first brashly expressed to my mother all those years earlier: *Real police work in the city.*

Of course, whenever I used that line on my higher-paid brothers and sisters in blue, their comeback was always: "Yeah, but smart ones work in the county."

I couldn't argue with that. No one else who did my job could, either.

Finally, though, my dad had had it up to here with all my complaining.

"Stop bitching and *do* something about it," he told me. "Nobody's gonna give you the stuff you deserve. You gotta go out there and *get* it."

So I did.

Following in the footsteps of my firefighter dad and brother, both of whom had been active in their union, I ran for a vice-president's slot in the Fraternal Order of Police and won.

The FOP was the union model I liked. It wasn't run by

union bosses. We weren't Teamsters. We weren't striking. We weren't run by organizers. But we *were* advocating. We were rank-and-file cops standing up for rank-and-file cops.

The more I worked with the FOP and the more I was around cops and their families, the more something else began to trouble me: leadership in the department was completely inept when it came to dealing with tragedies, such as the shooting or killing of a police officer.

Cops were good at putting on these solemn, elaborate and ritualized funerals you see often—far *too* often—on TV. But they were terrible when it comes to summoning the kind of compassion and succor police families needed in the aftermath of these awful events.

This was also not just a problem in Baltimore—it was an issue in police departments all over the country. All of them wrestled with the same over-arching concerns: How do we take care of families that are now in crisis? What can we do to help them through this process, from the initial notification that something horrible has occurred to their loved one all the way through to the final outcome, whether it was good or bad?

In particular, I saw a need to be there with the shocked and reeling families in the first 24 to 48 hours after a shooting or killing had occurred.

Everybody knew the command staff of a police department already had plenty on its plate in the immediate aftermath of these incidents.

The top brass had to deal with the politicians who wanted an accounting of what had just occurred. They had to deal with the media clamoring for details about the shooting. And finally, they had a horrific crime itself that had to be investigated. So those were the areas in which they were focused.

Their focus wasn't in holding a grieving widow's hand when she needed it most, one of the hardest jobs in the world. It wasn't in hugging an anguished family member as he or she sobbed uncontrollably.

I saw a need for somebody to step in and provide that kind of support and empathy from the moment the tragedy unfolded. And command was more than willing to turn that role over to the FOP—and by extension to me.

Soon, if I needed a food tray delivered with sodas and water to a hospital or a grieving family's home, I had a dedicated credit card to use so as not to get mired in a mountain of bureaucratic paperwork that needed to be filled out. Same thing if there was a family with a lot of out-of-town members—aunts, uncles, grandparents, etc.-- who quickly needed hotel rooms in Baltimore.

We made sure Maryland Shock Trauma, the world-renowned hospital where severely-injured officers are often treated, provided a dedicated staff that would give us periodic updates on the condition of the officer.

We also needed dedicated rooms and hallways where the worried and anxious families of the wounded officers could gather. And we needed other dedicated spaces for the deluge of cops who invariably converged on Shock Trauma when one of their own was shot, a place where they could unite and cry, hug and support each other—and not get in the way of the doctors and nurses working feverishly on the officer fighting for his life.

Finally if an officer were to die from his injuries, the FOP, along with the police department, would coordinate all the details of the funeral.

Police funerals are unique in terms of where the hearse is

located in the funeral procession. In a traditional funeral, the hearse is the first vehicle leaving the church or funeral home for the ride to the cemetery. In a police funeral, the hearse is the last vehicle.

This is done to minimize the time the grieving family has to spend at the cemetery. The funeral processions for fallen officers can go on for miles; it wouldn't do to have the family arrive first and then wait an hour and a half or more for the rest of the cortege to appear.

By putting the hearse last, the family could wait at the church or funeral home and have access to bathrooms and a chance to breathe a little after what was always an emotionally-wrought service.

For a full honors funeral, which is what the department oversees in virtually all line-of-duty deaths, the FOP would sit down with the family of the deceased officer and go over the many options for the ceremony.

These might include everything from bagpipers, a 21-gun salute, the release of butterflies or doves, or a fly-over with helicopters. We would also help with writing eulogies, and with deciding on the music and songs they wished to hear.

I was still learning my new role in the union when two back-to-back tragedies provided a stark look at the unique needs of cop families in crisis.

11.

The Thin Blue Line
Bends, Not Breaks

Late summer of 1992 proved to be one of the most devastating periods in the history of the Baltimore Police Department.

Just before noon on Sept. 18, Officer James E. Young, 26, was shot at the Flag House Courts, a dreary public housing project consisting of three high-rise buildings and multiple low-rise units not far from the glittering Inner Harbor.

Young was in plainclothes when he responded to a report of a man armed with a gun at one of the high-rises. After climbing the stairs to the third floor, the young officer was jumped in a dimly-lit hallway by a 21-year-old man named Sean Lamont Little, who wrestled Young's 9 mm Glock handgun away from him and shot him in the head.

Flag House was notorious for crime and violence; poverty and drug-dealing were rampant. Less than a month earlier, a team of police officers had been pinned down by snipers firing from one of the buildings and had to be extricated by an armored vehicle.

Still, the attack on Young was shocking for its brazenness and viciousness. It also underscored the difficulty of policing the tall buildings and vast canyons of complexes like Flag House, where then-Baltimore mayor Kurt Schmoke noted: "What we have is every social problem imaginable concentrated here."

Jimmy Young was rushed to Shock Trauma in critical condition. As soon as I received a page informing me of the shooting, I hurried over there, too.

What I remember most about that chaotic afternoon was the incredible number of officers that showed up to support Jimmy. Many milled outside the hospital, talking quietly among themselves and consoling one another.

My job was also to try to keep all these cops away from the TV news crews that routinely descend on Shock Trauma after an officer's been shot. The cameramen, we know, have a job to do: they're looking for footage of officers weeping and hugging to go along with the stories of the shooting that will air that night on the local stations.

But with emotions so raw and nerves so jangled, these cop-media interactions can be explosive.

Following any shooting of one of their own, cops are hurting. And they're angry. No, make that furious. They're furious at the shooter, furious that maybe a botched tactical plan got one of their fellow officers shot, furious at the revolving-door court system that lets so many criminals back out on the streets early.

And nothing will make them snap quicker than a member of the media shoving a microphone and a camera in their face and asking something asinine like "How do you feel?"

Clearly, the answer is: "Not too fucking good, buddy." It's written all over their drawn and ashen faces. Yet that kind of dumb question is posed to them all the time.

We were at the hospital for hours after Jimmy Young was shot. Many of his family and friends waited anxiously, many sobbing and praying as chaplains from both the police department and the hospital circulated quietly among them.

Periodically, a trauma surgeon would give us an update on Jimmy's condition, which remained critical. Doctors would discover the bullet went through his head, but that bone fragments had pierced his brain and caused considerable damage.

The shooting would cause him to have no memory of the attack itself. All he'd remember about that fateful day was pulling up to the Flag House projects and getting out of the car. It would also leave him brain-fogged, partially paralyzed and nearly blind.

"I only have peripheral vision," he testified nine months later at the trial of the drug dealer who shot him. "I can't see out the front at all. I can see out the side, but it is still very blurry."

As upsetting as the shooting of Jimmy Young was, it was quickly followed by another horrific incident that again left the entire department reeling.

Less than 24 hours after the attack on Young, another police officer, Ira Weiner, 28, was grievously wounded in a West Baltimore row house. In a tragic coincidence, he, too, was shot in the head by his own gun.

Weiner, who had been on the force only four years but was well-respected, had responded to a call about a disorderly armed man. Entering the house, he encountered a 29-year-old named Lewis Thomas Jr., whom relatives said was high on crack and acting paranoid.

Brandishing an ice pick, Thomas stabbed Weiner over the left eye. After wrenching the officer's gun from its holster and shooting him, Thomas reportedly shouted to relatives: "I'm ready to die. I'm dead already."

When other officers arrived outside the house, Thomas refused to surrender. When they burst through the front door, he shot at them and was killed in the return fire.

As with Jimmy Young, Ira Weiner was rushed to Shock Trauma. Having two critically-injured officers and their families there at the same time was completely overwhelming at first, although we quickly adjusted.

Right away, though, we were hearing that as serious as Jimmy's wounds were, Ira's were even worse. Soon the doctors were telling us that the bullet had penetrated his skull, and that bone and bullet fragments had done so much damage to his brain that it was too risky to operate.

We also heard the grim news that he was on life-support systems.

I met with Ira's mother, Arlene Weiner, who was, of course, devastated over what had happened to her only child.

It was my first time up close with the mother of a wounded police officer, and it was a sobering experience. Arlene would prove to be an incredibly strong woman. Yet sitting in a chair, with me kneeling on one knee beside her, she talked at length about how worried she often was when her son was at work.

The conversation made me think of my own mother, and how she might deal with a similar tragedy if something were to happen to her firefighter son, Tom, and her police officer son, Gary.

"I'm so sorry. We're here for you," I told Arlene over and over again, words that could sound so empty and insufficient in times of such wrenching grief.

I always tried to reassure the family members of the wounded that we were in the best place in the whole world for their loved one to be treated. As *the Washington Post* wrote about Shock Trauma, the nine-story complex near Baltimore's Camden Yards, this was "the nation's largest life-saving factory," having treated some 40,000 critically-injured patients at the time.

"If anybody can make a difference, it's the people here," I would say.

That's how I always framed it in talking to the families of injured cops. I never said the words "If anybody can *save* him..."

I didn't want to give the families any false optimism. But I wanted to reassure them that everything possible was being done for their loved one.

The families of police officers are almost always stunned at the overwhelming support they receive when a loved one is shot. The truth is, these families don't have a clue about what being in this "Blue Family" means until a tragedy of this magnitude happens.

This is usually their first time dealing with us as an agency since their loved one graduated from police the academy, with all the attendant pomp and circumstance of that event. Now there are non-stop food deliveries arriving, hotel arrangements being made for them, officers volunteering to pick up their family members at the airport.

Now there is all this high-ranking police brass in their midst and the mayor, police commissioner, city council members and droves of politicians stopping by to console and encourage them.

I was there at the hospital until well past midnight the next two nights as we all kept a grim watch on Jimmy and Ira. Finally at 12:01 a.m. on Sept. 21, Ira Weiner was taken off life-support at the request of his father. At Weiner's beloved Western District, the mood was both somber and reflective.

As reported by the *Sun*: "The message of Officer Weiner's death went out with the usual efficiency of any police department, and, like thousands of other broadcasts, it went out loud and clear.

"Preceded by an attention signal, the message (was): 'I regret to inform you that Officer Ira Weiner passed away at 0017 hours [12:17 a.m.] Our prayers are with our fellow officer.'

"Officers beginning the midnight-to-8 a.m. shift and those whose 8-hour shift just ended took out their elastic black mourning bands and placed them around their badges."

Weiner, of course, was given a full police funeral. I remember standing in the street outside the Sol Levinson funeral home on Reisterstown Road in full uniform with scores of my fellow officers, the crowd of mourners so vast we had no chance of getting inside.

Yet within days, I realized that responding to both of these crises in the role of FOP leadership, with the responsibility of taking care of family members and fellow officers of our injured and dying brothers, had brought me a great sense of duty.

While cops on the street often feel they have no control of many situations, I felt there was one thing we could control —and that was how we handled taking care of each other and the families of our fallen.

In my role as FOP vice-president, I felt like a leader. I felt like I was taking control and able to give orders even without having any rank—orders that everyone listened to because they all wanted to help.

Being there for each other was so important. And it made me further understand what we called "the Thin Blue Line." If we in law enforcement were the vaunted thin line that keeps society from descending into chaos, then we sure as hell had a massive responsibility to have each others' backs when things went sideways.

Soon, this is what drove me to consider putting my plans of a career as a homicide detective on hold. I had a more immediate goal now. My sights were set on a position I was uniquely qualified for, and one I was convinced would best serve the police department and— more importantly—my brother and sister officers.

I wanted to lead the FOP.

12.

Who Stands Behind Our Badge?

I launched my campaign to be the FOP president in the summer of 1993 with the over-arching theme: "Cops representing cops."

Central to this was the idea that having the police union led by a rank-and-file cop, as opposed to the sergeants and lieutenants who normally held the office, could only benefit the 80 percent of membership that was rank-and-file.

My main competition was a colorful and outspoken lieutenant named Chuck Milland. Four years earlier, Milland had written an article for Gallery, a seedy men's magazine, with the not-so-subtle title: "Why Cops Hate You." Predictably, his supervisors were less than thrilled with both the prose and the less-than-scholarly publication in which it appeared.

They were just getting over that when Milland lobbed another figurative hand grenade in their midst. In a 1992 piece for the *Sun*, he basically ripped what he perceived to be the namby-pamby judges causing crime to soar in the city. And he called for suspending the Constitution for a month so the cops could clean up the mess the feckless judicial system had made.

"Modern criminals have no fear of incarceration," he wrote. He called on citizens to tell their representatives at City Hall that for 30 days, "No complaints against police officers will be entertained by the Police Department for frisking suspicious people on the streets or for searching vehicles suspected of containing drugs or weapons."

Add to all this the fact Milland made no secret of his frequent forays to The Block, Baltimore's notorious downtown stretch of bars, strip clubs and sex shops, and the man could be a handful for the most sympathetic of bosses. (Milland was also one of the few cops on the force who was also an attorney; he told people the strippers he visited on The Block were his law clients.)

Yet Milland was enormously popular within the department. He was also a terrific cop and an excellent shift commander. But, again, he was a lieutenant, which played perfectly into my us-against-them appeal for support from ordinary cops.

By this time, too, I was starting to make my bones with the membership as second vice-president. I was doing the grunt work of bringing the grievances filed by my fellow cops—about unfair treatment, discrimination, pay and overtime issues, etc.—to the command staff's attention.

I found I enjoyed advocating for my fellow officers. But there were perils that came with the job, too. I was just 32 year old, and there were many in senior command positions—old-school guys—who were not about to let some young, snot-nosed cop tell them all the things they were doing wrong in dealing with their troops.

This was underscored vividly one day when I found myself going over one particular officer's grievance with a colonel named Leon N. Tomlin.

Tomlin was a bear of a man and an absolute legend in the department. He was also someone I greatly respected. He had risen through the ranks after his stellar work fighting drug traffickers in the 1970's, when he helped send heroin dealers like Melvin "Little Melvin" Williams, John E. "Liddie" Jones and James Wesley "Big Head Brother" Carter to prison.

Just a year earlier, as he drove to a doctor's appointment in an unmarked police cruiser, Tomlin had witnessed a man leaping from the trunk of a moving car in mid-town. This, of course, was not something you see every day, even in a crazed city like Baltimore.

The man leaping from the trunk was a jeweler named Douglas Legenhausen. He'd been forced into the trunk at gunpoint and taken hostage by a low-life named Dontay Carter, already wanted for murder.

Tomlin jumped out of his car and joined other cops in chasing and arresting Carter, which only served to further burnish the colonel's towering reputation as a "cop's cop."

In any event, this was the man I stood before in his office on the eighth floor of police headquarters as I explained the niggling grievance of an officer who'd been transferred to the Evidence Control Unit and hated his new assignment.

I knew I didn't have a great case. But it was my job to argue it nonetheless.

Yet as soon as we started the meeting, Col. Tomlin stood and walked over to the window that overlooked busy Fayette

Street below. As I talked, he kept gazing out the window with his back turned to me.

Finally I mustered the courage to say: "Colonel, what are you doing? I'm talking to you..."

At which point he finally turned around, looked me dead in the eye and said: "I'm trying to see where you're gonna land when I throw your ass out this window."

Was I intimidated? You bet.

Tomlin was a departmental icon who'd come through the ranks at time when cops in Baltimore didn't even *have* a union. (After the infamous 1974 police strike, which lasted four days, then-Commissioner Donald Pomerleau had revoked the union's bargaining rights and fired its organizers, eventually leading to the FOP being officially recognized as the representative of city cops.)

Now here I was, a young cop questioning the colonel's right as a superior officer to do whatever the hell he wanted to do.

Stunned by his remarks, all I could do was stammer "Thank you, sir, for your time" and leave before he saw me peeing in my pants. But while I'd been intimidated, I wasn't terrified. By this point I knew I could handle the rigors of leading the FOP and the often-tense back-and-forth negotiations with command—whether anyone there liked me or not.

Looking for counsel and support in my run for the presidency, I assembled a team of guys who had been active in the FOP. Our strategy was to treat my bid like a political campaign, with outreach poll workers and advocates in each of the nine police districts and all the specialized units.

I also developed a plan to hit every roll call in each district to get my name in front of as many cops as I could and explain the platform on which I was running. This included visiting the detail of some 40 or 50 officers from all over the city who volunteered to provide security during Orioles games at Camden Yards, which was sold out nightly in those days.

We held a fundraiser, a bull-and-oyster roast at which we auctioned off a Cal Ripken, Jr. autographed baseball and a Brady Anderson autographed bat, as well as posters of the shirtless, well-muscled O's outfielder that women swooned over.

We also made sure there were some 500 1-oz. bottles of Tabasco sauce available for those attending. Yes, there was a reason for this largesse.

Tabasco is a trademarked product—you could look this up—of the Louisiana-based McIlhenny Company. So what if the name was spelled differently than mine? While swilling beer and pouring dollops of the spicy red sauce on their pit beef or oysters, maybe my fellow cops would spot the McIlhenny on the label and think of me.

Just as in your typical political campaign, our bid for attention had no boundaries. We had thousands of McLhinney for President black ink pens with the FOP logo made up and distributed to officers, who accepted them gratefully as they were required to write up their reports only in black ink.

We made sure McLhinney for President key chains found their way into every police car in the city. And we produced laminated McLhinney for President calendars that cops could put in their "look-out books," the little notebooks that informed them of crimes that had occurred on their posts and a description of the suspects involved.

All of this stuff was unprecedented for an FOP election. The whole thing was exciting. I was the youngest guy running, and I thought I could outwork everyone else. In the closing weeks of the campaign, we mailed out two different brochures to the 5,000 or so active officers and retired FOP members who could vote.

One brochure featured a picture of me in my police uniform. Another showed a photo of an officer's badge on the front cover and the question: "WHO STANDS BEHIND OUR BADGE?" Inside was a photo of me and my bio and the bullet-points of the issues I hoped to tackle if elected.

One last bit of important business remained: I sent out a targeted letter to FOP retirees in which I again pledged to strengthen their pensions and health care, the only two issues they really cared about.

The FOP is unique in that retirees have "full voice and vote." They were a key target demographic for my campaign—or for anyone hoping to lead the union. I sensed these retirees voted in significantly higher numbers than active members, and that they regularly (and enthusiastically) attended their retirement meetings, too.

By the end of the campaign, I was physically and mentally drained. The FOP election was conducted solely via mail-in ballots. The ballots went out to membership in August and were counted in September at the FOP hall in Hampden. And so it was that around 10 o'clock on the evening of September 26, 1994, after the regular monthly meeting was held, the results of the voting were finally announced.

To say I was floored is an understatement.

With well over 3,000 ballots returned, I had won by an almost 2-to-1 margin, a much wider margin than I'd anticipated. All the hard work had paid off. I was now the youngest Baltimore City FOP president of all time. And the first rank-and-file guy to hold that post in almost 30 years.

Amid all the congratulations, I found a pay phone and called my dad to share the good news. The pride in his voice was unmistakable. I was proud too, of course. Yet even as we celebrated with a few drinks, I couldn't help thinking of the daunting task that lay before me.

The Police Department was in turmoil and its nearly 3,000 police officers were uneasy. A new commissioner, Thomas C. Frazier, had been brought in a few months earlier to reform the department and have it focus on community policing.

Frazier had been plucked from the police department in San Jose, Calif., after a 27-year-career in which he'd risen up through the ranks. Yet San Jose was a much smaller city than Baltimore, and many wondered if a West Coast chief was the right pick to oversee a bustling East Coast agency in a place with all the usual urban ills that made policing so difficult.

In his short time here, the new PC had not exactly ingratiated himself with the rank-and-file cops. They were already calling him "TV Tom" for his perceived showboating ways. And he was pushing this highly-controversial idea of rotating officers into other assignments—for example, putting homicide officers back in patrol and moving experienced narcotics detectives into other units.

I sensed I might have a hard time dealing with our new boss when I officially took over as FOP head in October.

But before I could tackle any issues of concern to my brothers and sisters in blue, I was involved in a wild incident that could have ended my career in a heartbeat.

After a long, grueling and nerve-wracking campaign, this was exactly what I didn't need.

13.

Denim Skirt and Cowboy Boots

Three days before taking over my new dream job, I received a call from the vice sergeant in the Southern District.

His unit was responding to complaints from the citizens of Brooklyn, in south Baltimore, about the surge in prostitution in their neighborhood. A "special operation" was underway to get the hookers off the streets—at least for a while.

But the sergeant had a problem.

"All our guys are pretty well-known down there," he said, referring to his undercover officers who could pose as johns. "Can you come help us out?"

"Okay," I replied, probably a little too quickly.

Technically, I was still a detective in narcotics. And this assignment would allow me to make overtime pay, something I wouldn't be able to do as FOP president.

Not only that, but I had the perfect vehicle for the "special operation." It was a "seized car," one used in a crime and now in the possession of law enforcement, and one I hadn't yet turned back in.

In fact, I had grown to love the car, a snazzy champagne-colored 500 series BMW. Well, *snazzy* if you could overlook the two bullet holes in the driver's side headrest. Oh, and the bullet mark on the trim that lent it just the right touch of bad-boy intrigue.

That evening I drove down to Brooklyn, near Patapsco Avenue, and met the sergeant and his squad.

"They're all out tonight," he said of the prostitutes swarming the area. "Go grab us five or six and you're done for the night."

Piece of cake, I thought, somehow forgetting that hardly anything in police work is ever a piece of cake.

Yet fortune smiled on me at first. Posing as a horny businessman in a coat and tie and shadowed by back-up surveillance teams driving around with me, I picked up one hooker after another in quick succession.

When each got in the car, we'd negotiate the deal. Then I'd drive to a desolate locale near some abandoned railroad tracks where the sex act was ostensibly to be consummated.

Even before the detectives materialized to arrest them, most of the "girls" sensed this was a "date" that was about to go sideways, and they gave us no trouble. Some of them actually looked relieved. The squad looked happy with the results, too.

It was, by any measure, a tidy operation all around.

Around 6:30, just as it was starting to get dark, I brought back my fifth hooker, hoping this might be the end of my work day. But no, that would have been too easy.

"Go get us one more," the sergeant pleaded, explaining he wanted me to look for a notorious hooker they'd been trying to bust for a while.

"Aw shit, all right," I replied.

It was always hard to turn down a request from a fellow brother in blue. Especially now that I was poised to lead the union and needed to remain in the good graces of as many of my fellow officers as I could.

They gave me a description of the infamous hooker: middle-aged, wearing cowboy boots, a denim skirt, denim vest, denim jacket and a white cowboy hat.

Holy hell! I thought. *What is this?!*

"You can't miss her," they said.

Apparently not. Unless she slips into a bar and masquerades as a country singer.

I drove up and down the streets for quite a while, trying to find her. Finally, I spotted her on a corner. When I pulled over, she jumped in the car. And that's when all the drama began.

From the moment I looked in her eyes, I could see she was crazy. So crazy that we didn't make a deal, didn't set a price, didn't talk about this sex act or that one. No matter what I said, she responded with a torrent of gibberish, waving her hands in the air like a madwoman.

Finally, I couldn't take it anymore.

"Get the hell out of my car!" I shouted.

Which is when a very, very bizarre encounter got much, much worse.

Fumbling in the huge handbag she was carrying, she pulled out what can only be described as an industrial-sized can of Mace. It was the biggest can of Mace I'd ever seen, enough to cover me from head to toe.

I wasn't about to just sit there and get a blast of this stuff. Grabbing my gun from under the seat, I flung the driver's-side door open and rolled out. The hooker leaped out of the car too, still brandishing the Mace and continuing to jabber incoherently.

Over the roof of the car, I pointed my gun at her and shouted: "DROP THE FUCKING MACE!"

Would it surprise you to know this woman did not take direction well?

"YOU ROTTEN BASTARDS!" she screamed. "YOU FUCKING GUYS ARE ALL ALIKE!"

At this point, we were doing this bizarre little dance around the car, circling each other warily while I shouted for her to drop the Mace and she kept ranting and raving. And the whole time I was thinking: *I'm gonna shoot this crazy-ass bitch! And I'm gonna be the FOP president in a matter of hours!*

A few seconds later, though, I heard what sounded like the quick toot of a horn. Like someone toggling a siren. Stealing a glance in the direction of the noise, I saw my back-up guys in the parking lot of a nearby 7-Eleven, leaning on an unmarked car and laughing their asses off.

Instantly it became clear: the whole thing with this nutjob was a set-up. As soon as I could safely do it, I jumped in the car and tore ass out of there.

"YOU GOOFY SONS OF BITCHES, I ALMOST KILLED THAT BITCH!" I railed at the back-up team when we all met up again.

Only then did I get the full story behind their little caper.

It turned out that the woman in the cowboy get-up wasn't even a hooker. She was just a local looney-tunes who walked around babbling to herself and blowing up at people on the street. Naturally, the backup guys thought it would be great fun to see her go Chernobyl when I approached her.

These crack detectives were also blissfully unaware that the woman carried around a can of Mace the size of a fire hydrant. But if they had any second thoughts about their little stunt, they didn't let on. In fact, the more I cursed them out, the more they laughed uproariously.

Finally, I had to laugh, too. Oh man, they got me good. Still, I couldn't help thinking about all the ways that encounter could have gone horribly wrong.

And how would it have looked on the future union prez's resume?

In his final act as a street cop, Officer McLhinney arrested five prostitutes and shot a deranged woman in the middle of South Baltimore as a result of a prank orchestrated by his fellow cops.

At that moment, taking over the FOP was looking more and more like the right career move for me.

Photographs

That's me holding a toy rifle with my buddies outside our Waverly home in 1966. Like many houses in the neighborhood, ours was decorated in orange and black to celebrate our beloved Orioles, who beat the Los Angeles Dodgers in the World Series that year.

My first day wearing the official Baltimore Police Department cadet uniform in June of 1980.

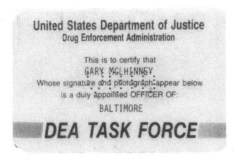

United States Department of Justice
Drug Enforcement Administration

This is to certify that
GARY MGLHINNEY.
Whose signature and photograph appear below
is a duly appointed OFFICER OF:

BALTIMORE

DEA TASK FORCE

OFFICE OF THE ADMINISTRATOR
Drug Enforcement Administration

My Baltimore DEA Task Force credentials from 1992, when we were investigating high-level narcotics dealers.

Rapper Ice-T flipping off Gene Cassidy in Hollywood in July 1992. Gene and other officers visiting the area had attempted to take Ice-T's picture. The artist, who had just released a controversial new track called "Cop Killer," apparently didn't like the idea.

Providing security for Orioles' legend Cal Ripken Jr. and his wife Kelly and children Rachel and Ryan at the parade in September 1995 to celebrate the Iron Man's breaking of Lou Gehrig's MLB record of consecutive games played (2130.)

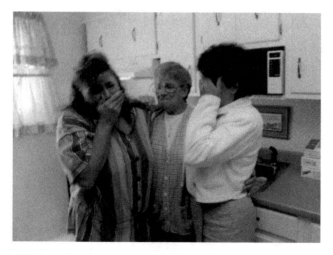

Hilda Adolfo (center) and daughters Janet Grossnickle (left) and Carol Miconi react to news of the Maryland Court of Appeals' decision in June 1996 to stay the execution of Officer Vincent Adolfo's killer, Flint Gregory Hunt. Credit: Baltimore *Sun*

Maryland's notorious gas chamber. Flint Gregory Hunt originally chose that form of execution before opting at the last minute for death by lethal injection in 1997.

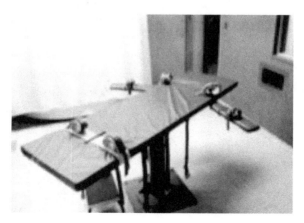

The table in the death chamber where Flint Gregory Hunt was put to death by lethal injection.

To Gary McLhinney
With Appreciation, Bill Clinton

Meeting Bill Clinton in November of 1998 before the president signed two addendums to the historic 1994 Crime Bill. As FOP president, I had been invited to
Washington to speak about the impact the new legislation would have on the safety
of police officers nationwide.

In March of 2000, I was invited to a news conference at City Hall where Mayor
Martin O'Malley discussed the resignation of Police Commissioner Ron Daniel and
the appointment of Ed Norris as acting commissioner.

With Mayor Martin O'Malley at a "roast" for me in May of 2000. The FOP had endorsed his opponent, Lawrence Bell, in the primary race. That's WBAL-TV's crack investigative reporter Jayne Miller in the bottom photo enjoying Martin getting his revenge by draping me with a spiffy "Vote Bell" T-shirt.

With New York City mayor Rudy Giuliani in the fall of 2002. Rudy had come to Baltimore to speak at a campaign event for gubernatorial candidate Bob Ehrlich. In violation of protocol, we arranged for the mayor's helicopter to land on the roof of Police Headquarters, which would have sent Mayor O'Malley into conniptions if he had found out beforehand.

Sensing a Bob Ehrlich victory, I joined the Republican candidate (gesturing in suit, white shirt and red tie) and dozens of his supporters for last-minute campaigning on the eve of the 2002 gubernatorial election in which he beat Democrat Kathleen Kennedy Townsend.

In my role as Maryland Transportation Authority Chief of Police, meeting George W. Bush in July of 2005 when he toured the Port of Baltimore. In a speech, the president encouraged the renewal of provisions of the Patriot Act, the anti-terrorism law enacted after the Sept. 11, 2001 attacks.

Addressing the media with Gov. Ehrlich by my side in October of 2005. This was the day when, as chief of the MdTA police, I ordered the closing of the Fort McHenry and Harbor tunnels during a terrorist investigation by the FBI. Credit: MdTA police.

With MdTA Police Officer Mike Dunn and Elaine Sweeny at Fallen Heroes Day at Dulaney Valley Memorial Gardens in May 2006. Elaine's husband, Baltimore Police Lt. Owen Sweeney Jr., was killed in May 1997 by a mentally-ill man wielding a shotgun. Mike Dunn was shot three times during a traffic stop in 1979; the driver of the vehicle had kidnapped and raped two women earlier in the evening.

With Gov. Ehrlich and my wife, Karen Kruger, at a fundraiser for the Maryland chapter of the Cystic Fibrosis Foundation at The Saint Paul's School in 2008. I had served on the chapters board of directors.

Never Forget

The following officers were killed in the line of duty during my years as FOP president and chief of the Maryland Transportation Authority Police.

Corporal Robert T. Krauss
Maryland Transportation Authority Police
EOW: Wednesday, December 21, 2005

Police Officer Harold Jerome Carey
Baltimore City Police Department, MD
EOW: Friday, October 30, 1998

Officer Grant F. Turner
Maryland Transportation Authority Police
EOW: Saturday, July 16, 2005

Lieutenant Owen Eugene Sweeney, Jr.
Baltimore City Police Department, MD
EOW: Wednesday, May 7, 1997

Officer Duke G. Aaron III
Maryland Transportation Authority Police
EOW: Tuesday, July 20, 2004

Police Officer Herman A. Jones, Sr.
Baltimore City Police Department, MD
EOW: Wednesday, May 26, 1993

Detective Thomas G. Newman
Baltimore City Police Department, MD
EOW: Saturday, November 23, 2002

Police Officer Ira Neil Weiner
Baltimore City Police Department, MD
EOW: Monday, September 21, 1992

Police Officer Crystal Deneen Sheffield
Baltimore City Police Department, MD
EOW: Thursday, August 22, 2002

Police Officer William J. Martin
Baltimore City Police Department, MD
EOW: Tuesday, October 10, 1989

Agent Michael Joseph Cowdery, Jr.
Baltimore City Police Department, MD
EOW: Tuesday, March 13, 2001

Police Officer Robert Alexander
Baltimore City Police Department, MD
EOW: Saturday, September 20, 1986

Police Officer Kevin Joseph McCarthy
Baltimore City Police Department, MD
EOW: Saturday, October 14, 2000

Police Officer Richard Thomas Miller
Baltimore City Police Department, MD
EOW: Monday, July 21, 1986

Sergeant John David Platt
Baltimore City Police Department, MD
EOW: Saturday, October 14, 2000

Police Officer Vincent J. Adolfo
Baltimore City Police Department, MD
EOW: Monday, November 18, 1985

Police Officer Kevon Malik Gavin
Baltimore City Police Department, MD
EOW: Friday, April 21, 2000

Police Officer Richard J. Lear
Baltimore City Police Department, MD
EOW: Tuesday, October 8, 1985

Police Officer Jamie Allen Roussey
Baltimore City Police Department, MD
EOW: Wednesday, March 8, 2000

Detective Marcellus Ward
Baltimore City Police Department, MD
EOW: Monday, December 3, 1984

Flight Officer Barry Winston Wood
Baltimore City Police Department, MD
EOW: Wednesday, November 4, 1998

Police Officer Ronald L. Tracey
Baltimore City Police Department, MD
EOW: Monday, July 20, 1981

14.

A Blind Cop Shows Us
The Way

On the night of my swearing-in as FOP president, in the late-summer of 1995, I was introduced to a sturdy-looking man in the audience with a vacant stare and a seeing-eye dog. The man's name was Gene Cassidy and he was already a legendary figure in the Baltimore Police Department.

On an Indian summer night in October eight years earlier, Gene, then a 27-year-old patrol officer in the Western district, attempted to arrest a man wanted on an assault warrant. The suspect, Clifton "Butchie" Frazier, 24, was no choir boy. He was a drug dealer and career criminal, the scourge of the neighborhood. Now he was wanted for beating up his 17-year-old girlfriend, Yolanda Marks, and then savagely pummeling an elderly man who had tried to intervene. (The man would lose his eye in the attack.)

According to eyewitness accounts later pieced together

by detectives, when Gene spotted Frazier walking with that same girlfriend along a desolate part of Appleton Street, he yelled "Hey, come here, pal!" After jumping from his patrol car and heading him off on foot, Gene jacked the younger man against a wall.

Frazier struck him in the chest with his elbow and simultaneously pulled out a .357 Magnum. The two struggled before Butchie managed to fire three shots at close range.

The first bullet ricocheted harmlessly off an alley wall. The second went through Gene's cheek, hitting his olfactory nerve and severing his right optic nerve. The third, fired with the gun rammed directly against Gene's temple, hit the back part of his eye and lodged in his brain.

Frazier fled the scene as his shocked girlfriend crumpled to the curb and wailed: "BUTCHIE SHOT A COP! BUTCHIE SHOT A COP!"

Gene was rushed to Shock Trauma, where surgeons operated on him for eight hours. He was given a four percent chance of survival. He stayed at University Hospital, and later at a rehab facility in Pennsylvania, for many weeks, defying the odds, the pain from his wounds and the stress of the horrific ordeal causing him to lose 50 pounds from his 6-foot frame.

Gene would be left with no memory of the shooting; the last thing he remembered about that fateful day was having hotdogs with his in-laws at their home in Hanover, Pa. Yet now he and his wife Patti, married just 13 months, dealt with the terrifying prospect that Gene, blind and unable to smell or taste, would remain that way for the rest of his life.

It was at University Hospital that doctors first told him he was unlikely to ever regain his sight. Of course, he and Patti sought a second opinion. After being examined at the world-renowned Wilmer Eye Institute at Johns Hopkins Hospital, Gene heard a voice say: "Well, Agent Cassidy, there's nothing we can do for you until the technology improves."

Gene thanked him quietly. When the man walked away, Gene turned to Patti and said: "Honey, don't worry. Wait 'til the doctor comes."

In a stricken voice, Patti replied: "Gene, that *was* the doctor."

On the car ride home from Hopkins that day, Gene told me, "there was an unbelievable trail of tears. We were both so totally devastated."

But not for long. Gene set a short-term goal: he wanted to be out of the hospital in time to celebrate Christmas in the home he and Patti had built—a beautiful Cape Cod with black shutters—in the Carroll County community of Millers.

Sure enough, he left the hospital on schedule. Then right before Christmas, Patti announced she was pregnant with their first child. The news triggered an outpouring of conflicting emotions in her still-reeling husband.

"How do you think I felt?" he asked when he told the story. "I was ecstatic! But I was also a little nervous. Like, how am I gonna do this?! How am I gonna change a diaper?!"

Gene's long-term goals were more opaque, even with a growing family to take care of.

He was only 27. With any luck, he had a long life in front of him. How was he going to support a wife and child? The gung-ho cop who averaged some 200 arrests a year was gone, and there was no bringing him back. But one thing he knew: he wanted to remain a police officer in some capacity.

The truth was, Gene had *always* wanted to be a cop. He carries a vivid memory of being an 8-year-old growing up in

Oakland, N.J., and seeing a police car racing down his street before pulling up to a neighbor's house, the officer grabbing his medical equipment and hustling inside.

That's what I want to do, Gene thought. *Help people like that.*

His father had been a World War II combat veteran—one of the famed Alamo Scouts, the U.S. Army's reconnaissance and raider unit that operated in the Pacific Theater—before taking a job with the federal government. Gene's mom was a registered nurse for 52 years.

Service to others was ingrained in the family. But had Butchie Frazier, the low-life who shot him, forever destroyed any chance of Gene remaining in his dream job?

"I didn't just *lose* my identity," he said of that horrible incident on Appleton Street. "It was ripped, torn and kicked away from me."

Butchie Frazier was eventually implicated by his old flame, Yolanda Marks, and arrested. He was convicted of first-degree attempted murder and sentenced to life in prison without parole.

At this point, Gene could have retired on 100-percent disability, with a full pension. But he and Patti had made a decision. They wanted their lives to return to a sense of normalcy as quickly as possible. And what was normal in Patti's world—she was a CPA at Citicorp, a rising star—and Gene's world was this: you get up every morning and go to work.

Even if you're now a blind cop.

No, there would be no sitting around the house, feeling sorry for himself and waiting for the disability checks to show up in the mail.

The police department offered him all kinds of desk jobs, including one working with computers, using what was described as cutting-edge, Braille-related equipment. But the thought of tapping away all day at a keyboard in the stultifying quiet of an office setting, especially given the darkness that now marked his world, didn't appeal to Gene one bit.

"I was like: that's not me," he recalled. "I could just see myself sitting there all day... getting bigger and bigger, eating dozens of donuts, drinking all the coffee I could... Nope, not my style."

Finally, he arrived at a decision: either the department would allow him to teach within their police academy—he had, after all, graduated from York College in Pennsylvania with a criminal justice degree—or he'd find a teaching job at a local high school.

The department agreed to his request. Gene ended up teaching a myriad of subjects, among them: law, moot court, post-shooting trauma, patrol techniques, HAZMAT issues and victimology, defined as the study of the psychological effects of crime and how victims and offenders interact.

He loved the new job from the very beginning. He was Agent Gene Cassidy now, not Officer Gene Cassidy. He wasn't carrying a gun and hitting the streets. But he was still a cop, still had his blue police ID card with his picture on it.

Within the department, he would go on to achieve almost mythic status. The story of the tragedy that nearly took his life and his remarkable recovery made its' way into David Simon's best-selling book "Homicide: A Year on the Killing Streets," and into a subsequent TV series "Homicide: Life on the Street."

He went back to school at Johns Hopkins and got his master's degree. And he found the idea of preparing young officers for the grueling demands of their job one of the most stimulating and rewarding things he had ever done.

"As a patrol officer, you want to learn your craft," he told me. "And I was (still) learning my craft. I was open-eyed and open-eared."

Over the years, Gene tirelessly instructed hundreds of new police recruits, even after he was diagnosed with Hepatitis C from the blood transfusions he was given during those first frantic hours when his ambulance screamed up to the doors of Shock Trauma.

But he survived that ordeal, too.

He spent months with his body so swollen and his feet so sore he couldn't walk. He became confused at times and struggled to piece together everyday conversations. But in 2012, Cassidy, now 57, underwent a liver transplant that doctors said saved his life.

I don't know of anybody in the long history of the Baltimore Police Department who has had such an impact on his fellow officers.

After that initial introduction at my FOP swearing-in, Gene and I became good friends. It turned out we lived in the same Bel Air community and had sons the same age. We'd run into each other at high school sports events and Ravens games, where Gene had become a huge fan of the team's ferocious middle linebacker, Ray Lewis.

Frankly, I was in awe of Gene.

To me, he was a living, walking example of the sacrifice you're forced to make sometimes in police work. To suffer the devastating injuries he suffered, and then not only to survive, but to *thrive*, and more importantly to give back to the department and the profession… to my mind that was the very definition of a hero.

Yet all of that was not enough to insulate Gene from the vagaries of City Hall politics and the whims of new leadership at police headquarters.

A few years after Tom Frazier was named commissioner, Gene began to sense that some in the department wanted him gone. Frazier was hell-bent on rotating officers through different jobs, even going so far as to propose moving veteran cops from the homicide, K9 and drug units back to patrol.

Frazier didn't care if a guy had 30 years on the job—he was going to put him back into a patrol car humping calls.

There was also a targeted effort to weed out those on the force considered permanent malingerers, as well as cops who were injured and collecting their full salary that could be pushed into retirement, where they'd be eligible for only two-thirds of their pay.

Yet Gene was a special case. He was so widely admired for all he'd gone through, all he'd overcome and all he'd given to the police academy, that command realized his case had to be handled with extreme sensitivity.

I recall Gene calling me into his office one day while I was attending in-service training. He asked me point-blank if the department was going to force him out. I told him there was no way in hell I was going to let that happen.

I knew that if they seriously attempted to kick him to the curb, I would have an army of 3,000 cops at my disposal to make their lives miserable. It would have been a labor war such as the department had never seen before, a message I also personally delivered to the police commissioner.

You couldn't bull-rush a cop like Gene, with that kind of legacy, out the door just to save a few bucks. So after couple of years of Gene ignoring cheerful comments about how much he might enjoy retired life—*You should think about it, Gene!*—command finally gave up the ghost.

Now the thinking was: *We can't do anything about Gene until Gene wants to go.*

And Gene didn't want to go. Gene wanted to continue to teach.

Which he did, masterfully and with great dedication, for a total of 24 years until finally leaving the force in November of 2015.

Not to retire. He was still not ready for that. To take a job with the FBI.

"The Police Department is losing an icon of public service," former commissioner Frederick Bealefeld told the *Sun*. But if there was a note of wistfulness in Bealefeld's remarks that day, there seemed to be none in Gene Cassidy's.

He seemed as steadfast and eager for new challenges as ever.

"It's closing one chapter and opening another," he told reporters. "The adventure continues forward."

15.

A Front Row Seat to a Singular Event

Late in the summer of 1995, the entire country seemed riveted by the drama unfolding around a 35-year-old shortstop for the Baltimore Orioles named Cal Ripken Jr.

Cal was on the verge of breaking one of the most hallowed records in all of sports: Lou Gehrig's major league mark for consecutive games played (2130), which had stood for 56 years. Anticipation had been building for months. And as we entered the first week of September in Baltimore, the white-hot media scrutiny "The Streak" had attracted, the heightened fan interest it inspired and the frenzy it set off among sports merchandise dealers and memorabilia collectors was overwhelming.

Cal, a native of nearby Aberdeen, Md., had been a hometown hero for many years, of course. But his quiet grit and the diligent, workman-like way he went about his job had inspired legions of new admirers everywhere. Many also credited him and "The Streak" with "saving baseball" following the disastrous player strike of 1994 that cancelled the World Series and left fans in a sour mood toward the National Pastime.

As the Orioles prepared to begin a three-game series against the California Angels at Camden Yards, during which Cal was expected to break Gehrig's record, I was approached by a friend of mine, Lt. Russell Shea.

Russ was the head of the stadium police detail. He told me he'd been hired to do security for Cal during "Streak Week." (As cops, we were allowed to moonlight, what we called "secondary employment.") He asked if I'd be interested in doing the same for Cal's wife, Kelly, and their two young children, Rachel and Ryan.

As a life-long Orioles fan who'd grown up in the shadows of old Memorial Stadium and watched Cal play since he won American League Rookie of the Years honors in 1982 and the league Most Valuable Player award the following season, I was thrilled with the opportunity to help the family. It really didn't matter that I would get paid, too.

The truth was, there were plenty of reasons for the Ripkens to be concerned for their safety.

Just a week earlier, as the Orioles played the Seattle Mariners on the West Coast, a man who identified himself as "Lou Gehrig Jr." had placed a telephone call to the Kingdome saying he would shoot and kill Cal if he played that night.

Law enforcement officials had downplayed the seriousness of the threat, chalking it up to another lunatic seeking the requisite 15 minutes of fame. (For the record, Gehrig had no children.) Ripken played all nine innings that night and was not told about the threat until after the game.

But the incident was unsettling. Two years earlier, also in Seattle, Cal had received another death threat, this time via computer from a teen-age girl. Police ultimately determined the girl was harmless; her story was that she'd meant to pull a prank on her boyfriend, a big fan of the All-Star infielder.

Still, Cal and his family had steadily watched their privacy erode and their world shrink as the Streak went on. Outings to movie theaters and restaurants took place only after the most meticulous planning to avoid attracting attention—or were cancelled altogether.

In an attempt to get some peace and quiet, Cal had been forced to stay in a different hotel from the rest of the Orioles when the team was on the road. Even though he used an alias when checking in, zealous fans often figured out where he was staying and roamed the floors, hoping to run into him.

Some had even knocked on his room door at all hours. Once, while getting ice at 12:30 in the morning in one hotel, he'd been startled when two memorabilia collectors who'd been stalking him jumped out from behind a soda machine.

Luckily, they were packing nothing more dangerous than Flair pens and Magic Markers. Nevertheless, Cal was spooked by the sudden presence of the two strangers. Who wouldn't be?

Now, with three sold-out games upcoming and Camden Yards expected to be packed with politicians, movie stars and famous ex-athletes—not to mention 40,000-plus roaring fans for the grand event—I was tasked with making sure Kelly and the kids stayed safe amid all the hoopla.

That Labor Day Monday, Sept. 4, Kelly, the kids and her mom and dad were driven to the ballpark in a chauffeured Chevy Suburban SUV. I rode with them, squashed into a cramped back-row seat.

Rachel and Ryan were restless. This was when I performed my first heroic act of body-guarding. When Kelly's dad, Bob Geer, started singing Barney the Dinosaur songs to entertain the kids, I thought: *Heck, my two boys are the same age. I've got the entire Barney oeuvre down pat.*

So I quickly introduced my mellifluous tenor to the proceedings and we happily sang Barney songs all the way down to the ballpark. Although the excitement level at Camden Yards was nearing fever pitch, with 42,086 raucous fans in the stands, the rest of the day was relatively uneventful for me. (And uneventful is definitely what you want when doing security work.)

I watched over the family in both their box and field seats, the Orioles lost to the Angels 5-3, and Cal homered and notched his 2129th consecutive game to pull within one of tying Gehrig's record.

Five-year-old Rachel started her first day at school the next day. Kelly drove her to St. Paul's School for Girls and I rode along with them. It was important to Cal and Kelly that Rachel have the kind of normal first day every child deserves.

Then again, how many kids have an off-duty policeman sitting in their classroom for three hours, the way she did that day?

Carrying a gun in a fanny-pack, no less?

Very few, I suspect.

The atmosphere was even more charged at Camden Yards that night, Sept. 5, when Cal went 3-for-5 with another homer in the O's 8-0 win as he notched consecutive game 2130. When he talked to the media at a little before midnight, though, his exhaustion was palpable.

"I'm looking forward to it," he said of finally breaking the Iron Horse's record. "And I'm looking forward to the end of it too, to be honest.... The last few days have been an eternity. Every time you look at the clock, it seems to move more slowly..."

Yet we all knew the evening was merely a dress rehearsal for the following night, Sept. 6, when the frenzy would reach a level never before seen at the most charming ballpark in all the land.

On the ride to Camden Yards that day with Kelly and the kids, I was feeling both stress and exhilaration. The strain of watching over my VIP charges was taking its' toll. But I was also thrilled to be having a front-row seat to history—providing I could actually get us into the place to *see* that history unfold.

I say this because as we neared the stadium, we were stuck at a red light as the motorcade of President Bill Clinton and Vice-President Al Gore—two of the many honored dignitaries expected to be on hand—appeared.

The motorcade seemed to stretch for miles. As car after car passed and we remained at a standstill, I was getting more and more anxious that we wouldn't get inside for the start of the opening ceremonies, in which Kelly and the kids were to play an integral role.

And guess who would have taken major heat for that screw-up?

Yes, your humble, newly-installed FOP head.

Finally, I rolled down the window and got the attention of the cop controlling traffic. I flashed my badge and explained the situation.

"Listen," I said, "I have Kelly Ripken and her kids here. We're late and we need to get inside. This game can start if the president's not here. It can start if the *vice-president's* not here.

"But it *can't* start," I continued, pointing to the children, whom I hoped were now striking a suitably angelic pose, "if *they're* not there. Because they're throwing out the first pitch."

Apparently, this logic was unassailable to my fellow brother in blue.

"No problem," he said. "I'll jump you in behind the ambo."

And so it was that we were whisked behind a city ambulance into the bowels of the stadium, ensuring that a) Rachel and Ryan could partake in the first-pitch ritual with their famous father from their box seats near home plate and that b) I would not be forever known as the guy who mucked up pre-game festivities that had been planned as meticulously as the D-Day invasion of Europe.

The rest of the evening played out like something out of a gauzy Hollywood movie. Certainly, it was one of the most emotional and joyous events the City of Baltimore had ever seen.

As he often did, Cal rose to the occasion, belting a line-drive homer over the left field wall in the fourth inning to give the Orioles a 3-1 lead over the Angels. And when the game became official after the top of the fifth inning and fireworks exploded and the huge illuminated numbers 2131 rolled down the side of the B&O warehouse, Cal took his now-legendary hand-shaking lap around the ballpark, basking in the love and admiration of the crowd of 46,272.

The 22-minute standing ovation was amazing. As Whitney Houston's "One Moment in Time" blared over the sound system, someone in the stands held up a sign that said: "We consider ourselves the luckiest fans on the face of the earth.

Thanks, Cal."

In a ceremony after the Orioles' 4-2 win, Cal marked the landmark game with a touching tribute to the legendary New York Yankee to whom he'd be forever be connected.

"Tonight, I stand here, overwhelmed, as my name is linked with the great and courageous Lou Gehrig," he said in a voice thick with emotion. "I'm truly humbled to have our names spoken in the same breath."

I took in all of this incredible drama from my perch behind Kelly and the kids in their field box.

Although I spent much of the time with my back to the field—if there was a threat to their well-being, it was more likely to come from the stands, of course—I felt both humbled and immensely fortunate to be on hand for arguably the most singular event in Baltimore sports history.

For a kid from Waverly, who wore his black and orange with pride, this was a day to be cherished forever.

16.

"The Big Guy's Upset!"

Thursday, Sept. 6, was an off-day for the Orioles, but my work for the Ripkens wasn't done yet.

A huge parade to celebrate Cal's historic achievement stepped off at noon from the Washington Monument. It wound its' way downtown past cheering throngs to the Inner Harbor, with Russ Shea and me on either side of the big float carrying Cal, Kelly and the kids.

(A photo of me on a float with Cal that appeared in The New York Times and Sports Illustrated, among other publications, was another thrill I could have never imagined growing up as a die-hard O's fan.

(On the other hand, I was told our new police commissioner, "TV Tom" Frazier, was going out of his mind seeing me all over the television and print media. We were in complete battle mode over several issues, the PC and I, with him actually calling me "the union punk" to his minions in the department.)

At the Harbor's edge, a dais had been set up on the deck of the Pride of Baltimore II, the famed replica of a 19th-century schooner. From there, Cal, various civic officials, Orioles brass and teammates would address the enormous crowd packed into the amphitheater at the confluence of Pratt and Light Streets.

Cal was drained from all the hoopla and fighting a brutal head cold. But when I looked out at the sea of happy faces and saw my son, Danny, perched on my dad's shoulders, both of them smiling radiantly, I pointed them out to Cal and he gave them a nice wave.

It was a moment I'll never forget. Neither will Danny and my dad. In fact, when my wife Sandy picked up Danny from pre-school a couple of days later, the teacher said to Sandy: "Danny told us the story about Cal Ripken being in his Daddy's parade!"

The ceremony went on for some time, even though Cal was scheduled to be honored at a similar parade in Aberdeen at 6 that evening. When it was over, the adoring masses, predictably, did not disperse right away. No one wanted the love-fest to end.

Yet as a result of some brilliant logistical planning, a way to extricate Cal had been devised. The Pride II simply pulled away from the dock and set sail to the other side of the harbor, where the cars and buses for the various big-shots had been parked.

Thus was Cal assured of getting to his hometown—a 45-minute trip north as the crow flies, but much longer if the crow is stuck in rush hour traffic on I-95—to be feted a second time.

Russ and I drove Cal to the airport the next day for his

flight to Cleveland, where the Orioles were to open a three-game series with the Indians. This was before the 911 tragedies, of course, and we managed to avoid the terminal and get him onto the tarmac and into his first-class seat through the use of an age-old psychological tactic that never fails: bribery.

A few baseballs with the Iron Man's autograph doled out to select airport personnel at the various gates did the trick.

If Cal was wiped out physically and emotionally at this point, my energy levels were not so great, either. I thought my stint doing security for the Ripkens was over. But after a quick overnight trip to Ohio for an FOP event that left me even more bleary-eyed, my phone rang Saturday morning.

On the other end was Desiree Pilachowski, one of Cal's assistants.

"We have a problem," she announced ominously. "Cal's out of town, Kelly's at the house and the alarm system's not working. Plus Champ the dog is sick."

There was a pause as I took all this in.

"I'd really like you to go out there to (provide security) overnight," she continued.

I groaned inwardly. Maybe outwardly too. By this point, I was too whipped to be sure where the groans were coming from.

"Normally, I'd say yes," I told Desiree. "But I haven't even been to bed yet. I gotta get some sleep."

In the past, whenever I watched the house, I'd make my rounds of the property and grab some shut-eye in my car before setting out to check the locks and gates again. But I knew I was far too exhausted for that now.

A nap in the Ripken driveway might put me out for hours. If there were any bad guys—or anyone else—looking to gain access to the premises, they'd be able to waltz right in to the soundtrack of one of Baltimore's finest snoring contentedly out front.

"OK," Desiree said, "let me call you back."

The phone rang a few minutes later.

"OK," Desiree said, "Kelly says you can stay in the guest room. That way you can get some sleep. And when you hear them up in the morning, you can just leave."

Sounds like a plan, I thought.

I got to the house around 9 that night. Kelly let me in and gave me a key. I did my usual patrol out by the pool and around the perimeter to make sure everything was secure. I even managed to get a little sleep that night. (Although I slept on top of the bedspread, afraid that if I got under the covers, I'd be so comfortable I'd never wake up again.)

The next morning, when I heard the family stirring upstairs, I let myself out. I was still dog-tired, but I went straight to the office to do some work. When I left at noon to go home, I got a phone call.

It was Desiree.

"We got a problem," she said.

Again?

Another problem?

"The big guy's upset," she went on. "We told him this morning that the house alarm was out, Champ was sick and you stayed over at the house. Anyway, he didn't think that was appropriate. He said you shouldn't have done it. He said you should have known better.

"And," she added, "he's gonna call you in a little while to discuss the whole thing."

When she hung up, my mind reeled.

What the fuck was this? Cal was pissed at me? For what? Hadn't Desiree all but implored me to stay over? Hadn't Kelly herself let me in and said she was glad I was there?

This was a few years before the wild and unsubstantiated rumors about Kelly fooling around with the actor, Kevin Costner,- and other men began circulating around Baltimore—vicious rumors I never believed in the first place.

So what was Cal all bent out of shape about?

For the better part of an hour, I went over every possible scenario in my head. By the time the phone rang again, I was a nervous wreck.

But the voice on the other end wasn't Cal's.

It was Desiree's.

"Gotcha!" was all she said.

"*What?*" I replied.

In my muddled state of mind, I couldn't process what I'd just heard.

"Gotcha!" she said again.

Only then did the thick brain-fog begin to lift. Only then did I realize that—once again—I'd been had.

"YOU SON OF A BITCH!" I shouted, as she began to cackle. "I *WILL* PAY YOU BACK! AND IT *WILL* INVOLVE HANDCUFFS!"

It was one of the best practical jokes ever played on me—and as a cop, I'd been a magnet for this stuff my entire career. Coming so soon on the heels of the crazy Brooklyn "cowgirl hooker" prank, this one probably led to a few more premature gray hairs—if it didn't actually take years off my life.

Which it probably did.

17.

Stepping Up For A Good Cop

As every police officer will tell you, there's no such thing as a "routine" traffic stop. It is the great myth that endures in the general public.

Each stop is stressful to some degree—depending on such variables as the time of day, the part of town where the stop occurs, the number of occupants in the vehicle, etc. All bring the vast potential for danger.

Police carry out some 20 million stops on streets and highways all over the U.S. each year. And on many of those stops, they approach the vehicle without any idea of who's behind the wheel and whether that person is armed, has committed a crime, or is mentally unstable.

On a winter evening in February 1996, Sgt. Stephen Pagotto, a 13-year-veteran of the BPD, came face-to-face with this reality in Northeast Baltimore when he pulled over a white

Subaru driven by a 22-year-old named Preston Barnes.

Pagotto was part of a unit tasked with getting guns off the street. He and his partner flagged Barnes' car when they noticed it had no rear license tag. Given the neighborhood they were in and the way the three young men in the car were moving about, Pagotto's instincts led him to suspect the car might also hold drugs or guns.

The stop, as these things can, quickly went south.

When Pagotto approached Barnes with his gun drawn and ordered him out of the car, Barnes hit the gas instead. When the sergeant tried to grab Barnes with his left hand, the officer stumbled and his gun accidentally fired. The bullet hit Barnes in the left armpit, killing him.

(Barnes was later found to be on probation for drug possession, and to have prior convictions on narcotics and handgun charges. Ten bags of crack cocaine were found in his car. Two of the passengers would admit they were hoping to sell drugs that evening, and that Barnes had an escape plan to "floor it" if stopped by the police.)

So much for a routine traffic stop...

I made it a point, if I was in town, to go to the scene of every police shooting, and this one was no different. I went because I knew how the trauma of these incidents could affect these officers—whether the shooting was accidental or not. And I wanted to assure the officers that everything would be OK.

People outside the department can't possibly know the emotional toll that comes when a cop is forced to pull the trigger in the line of duty. Or when someone dies in that officer's custody. Every cop reacts differently, of course.

Some are devastated and you know they're about to be

haunted by nightmares, or start reaching for the bottle. Others are seemingly less affected, or able to compartmentalize what they've just gone through, with an attitude that says: *OK, I'm good now. Gimme my gun back and let me get back to work.*

When I met Steve at Police Headquarters with our FOP attorneys after the shooting, he was quiet. Certainly, he understood the seriousness of what had just happened. But he also understood that he hadn't done anything wrong.

This was a horrible accident, his demeanor said. *Nothing more.*

I always told the officers involved in shootings not to turn on the TV when they got home later. Because we always knew what they were going to see. That night on the evening news, even if the officer had had an Uzi pointed at him that fired 30 rounds in five seconds, the shooter would be portrayed as a good person who was turning his life around and attempting to make something of himself.

It didn't matter if he was a choir boy or a 10-time convicted felon—that's what we were going to see. And we were going to hear from so-called witnesses who weren't anywhere near where the incident occurred and didn't see what happened, but wanted to be on TV.

So don't watch TV, I always told these cops. And don't let your families watch, either.

Quite frankly, from the preliminary info I heard about the incident involving Preston Barnes, I didn't think Steve had anything to worry about. *Yes, it was a terrible tragedy*, I thought. *But nothing's going to come of this.*

Within a few days, however, a police spokesman was telling the media that aspects of the Barnes shooting were "troubling." Pagotto was said to be non-cooperative with investigators looking into the incident. But this stemmed mostly from the advice of the FOP that officers involved in shootings talk with our lawyers before issuing any statements.

Steve was also said to be less than forthcoming when he first called in the shooting over his police radio, which of course could be attributed to the highly-adrenalized situation he'd suddenly found himself in.

In any event, it was clear to all of us in the FOP that Commissioner Frazier—among others on the command staff—was not going to back Steve Pagotto. Frazier was still early in his tenure running the department, already earning the distrust of the rank-and-file. But this would have been the perfect time to come out in support of one of his officers.

He didn't have to say: "Hey, my guy was great, he did everything right that night!" But he could have come out and explained the circumstances behind the Barnes shooting. He could have talked about what it was like to make the kind of high-risk stops Steve and his unit were making, and how the mandate was for them to go out there and get guns, be aggressive.

Instead, the silence from the commish was deafening.

The following month, Pagotto was indicted by a grand jury on a charge of manslaughter. He turned himself in, was processed and released on a $50,000 unsecured bond. Immediately, he was suspended without pay, another thing Frazier could have prevented.

The commissioner could have continued having Steve do administrative duties at headquarters . He could have announced: "Yes, we know there are a lot of questions surrounding this case. And we'll get to the bottom of it" while still keeping Steve employed.

I went to Frazier and personally appealed to him not to

take away Steve's paycheck. But it was futile. The commissioner saw which way the political winds were blowing. The racial dynamics of a white police commissioner defending a white sergeant who shot an African-American youth didn't escape him, either.

From that point on, the FOP went into defense mode for Steve, working with our lawyers and lining up the right experts to testify at his trial. Steve was facing a possible 10-year-sentence, and now the city was all whipped up.

The haters had a cop in their sights. They were practically salivating at the prospect of bringing him down. "Killer Cop Pagotto" was even scrawled on the family van parked at Steve's home.

Yet what happened next was amazing.

Within a matter of days after news of Steve's suspension broke, cash and checks earmarked for him began pouring in to the FOP. People would walk into our office to personally hand over donations. Soon we were able to match Steve's sergeant's salary, which was a great relief to him and his family.

Steve's trial began in late November, and we were confident he'd be exonerated. Our attorney, Henry Belsky, was a terrific trial lawyer, and he was in his prime here. Henry was a rumpled, Falstaffian figure, with a thick thatch of erratically-combed hair and remnants of his last meal invariably dotting his sports jacket or tie.

He was also a really smart guy who never came across as pompous or slick, and his down-to-earth demeanor helped him relate well to juries.

The prosecution focused its case on the way Steve had handled his 9 mm Glock handgun and the placement of his trigger finger during the traffic stop with Barnes. Also brought up was the fact Steve had reached into the car with one hand as it moved away, a technical violation of Police Department policies.

But Belsky hammered away on a central theme of Steve's defense: that Barnes, terrified of the cops finding his stash and being sent back to prison, had attempted to flee from the lawful detention of a police officer, essentially causing his own death.

Pagotto, Henry emphasized, had been doing what his superiors wanted him to do, "aggressively confront criminals to see if they had guns and to take them off them."

Yet after three weeks of testimony, Steve Pagotto was found guilty by a jury of involuntary manslaughter and two counts of reckless endangerment, thereby becoming, as the *Sun* reported, "the first city officer in memory to be convicted of a crime for shooting in the line of duty."

To say we were stunned by the verdict—and outraged—is an understatement. "I think it sends a very bad message—that it doesn't pay to do your job on the Baltimore police force," Henry Belsky told reporters. "It's better to sit back in the district and drink coffee."

The scary part of the prosecution for me was: how do I tell our officers on the street that now they can be charged criminally with violating a rule, or a tactic, or a policy? And as anyone with common sense knows, there's no rule, policy or tactic that can be taught at the police academy that can mimic every situation an officer confronts on the street.

For the academics in the policing world to think so, or for a police commander to think so… well, it just proves they've been off the street way too long. And they need to go back to see what it's like out there. And for the prosecutors to say, from the safety of their nice, cozy offices, that Steve should have had his trigger finger in *this* exact position, or that he shouldn't have reached into the car with his hand like *that* as it accelerated, is Monday morning quarterbacking at its most shameful.

And it's most dangerous.

Nevertheless, two months later, Steve was sentenced to three years in prison. Again, we were staggered, this time by the severity of the punishment. Henry Belsky had asked that Steve be sentenced to community service and not serve any time.

Before the sentencing, Steve had asked the judge for mercy and apologized profusely to Preston Barnes' mother, Sylvia Smith. But Circuit Court Judge John Carroll Byrnes was unmoved. Jail time, the judge said, would reiterate to the citizens of Baltimore and the police "that we continue to honor life's value."

As we had at the trial, the FOP had packed the courtroom with cops, all of us wearing distinctive blue ribbons to show our support of Steve. It was, to be sure, an emotionally-charged scene. When Judge Byrnes read the sentence, Steve grimaced and hung his head; he must have wondered if his life was over. Behind him, his wife and children sobbed. Our officers were outraged.

Naturally, Steve and our lawyers appealed the conviction; he was freed on a $75,000 bond pending the outcome. Five months later, on the recommendation of Henry Belsky, Judge Byrnes agreed to trim Steve's sentence to 20 months in prison.

But it would be two more years before the Maryland Court of Special Appeals would throw out his manslaughter conviction, finally giving him and his family a measure of comfort and hope after their long ordeal.

Pagotto, the court said in its ruling, had violated departmental rules and training guidelines. But his shooting of Preston Barnes was accidental, and not the result of criminal negligence.

The FOP and the Police Department were, of course, ecstatic over the decision. Not only did it save Steve from going to jail, it also set a pretty good precedent, in our minds, about how the courts would react with similar cases in the future.

"This is an important day for police officers," I told reporters when asked for my reaction. "Accidents should not cause people to go to jail, especially when you're asking officers to do jobs like get guns off the street. Criminals don't stop and throw up their hands and say 'You got me.'"

As for me personally, I was again proud to be the president of the FOP that day, grateful to head an organization that had gone to bat for a good cop unjustly accused of wrong-doing, an organization that had gone toe-to-toe with the judge when the Police Commissioner and much of the command staff wouldn't.

It was a solid victory for us. And it reiterated to our membership why we existed. A cop going through this tribulation on his own would have gone bankrupt, having to pay the enormous legal expenses without having a job and a paycheck.

From the very beginning, Steve Pagotto' defense had not cost him or his family a dime. So there was tremendous satisfaction in knowing we had been there for them in their darkest hour, when they needed us most.

As we suspected it might, the Maryland attorney general's office chose to appeal this latest ruling. But the following year, the state's highest court also ruled in Steve's favor, officially clearing him of manslaughter and putting an end to the whole nightmarish saga.

By then, Steve was working as a salesman at a car dealership. He talked of possibly returning to the police force, but never did. Yet the impact of his case on all the hard-working men and women in blue who hit the streets of Baltimore every day could not be overstated

Police officers, Henry Belsky told reporters, "now get a better break. No longer will they be second-guessed on every minor detail of what they did. (Instead) they will be given a little bit of latitude to protect themselves in dangerous situations."

None more dangerous, at times, than a "routine" traffic stop.

18.

Jesse Jackson Comes to Town

In the spring of 1996, it appeared as if the family of Vincent Adolfo would finally receive the justice for which they'd so long prayed. Flint Gregory Hunt, the career criminal who had cold-bloodedly gunned down the young Baltimore cop in a dreary East Baltimore alley nearly 12 years earlier, was now scheduled to die in the gas chamber the week of June 10.

Vince's family and his widow, Karen Adolfo, had endured unimaginable pain in the years since Vince was killed—much of it inflicted by the lugubrious court system.

Hunt had been convicted of first-degree murder and sentenced to die after his initial trial in 1986. But two years later, the Maryland Court of Appeals overturned the sentence after a U.S. Supreme Court ruling that victim impact statements presented to juries during death penalty sentencing hearings could taint the proceedings.

The deceased's family's expressions of grief and distress were irrelevant, the Supreme Court ruled. Juries should consider only the evidence presented at trial.

This, of course, was another huge blow for the Adolfo family. Months later, after deliberating for a little more than three hours, a Baltimore Circuit Court jury again sentenced Hunt to death. But the endless appeals and legal maneuverings on the part of Hunt's defense team in the eight years since had left the Adolfo family alternately enraged, saddened and exhausted.

Even now, as the execution date neared, they were wary of any last-minute machinations that would allow Hunt to again escape the gas chamber. At the FOP, so was I. And so were my brothers and sisters in blue.

It turned out we were right to be on high alert.

On the afternoon of Wednesday, May 29, my phone began ringing off the hook. Every media outlet in the state seemed to be calling.

I soon learned why: Jesse Jackson was coming to town.

The esteemed civil rights leader was planning a quick trip to visit Flint Gregory Hunt in his cell at Baltimore's Supermax prison. Rev. Jackson was also hoping to meet with Gov. Parris Glendening and persuade him to stop the execution, while also having the governor look into why there were so many blacks on Maryland's Death Row compared to whites.

At the FOP, our members, both black and white—this was a "Blue" thing, after all—were incensed that Jackson would inject himself into this case. Our focus quickly became: OK, how are we going to address this?

We knew from seeing different death penalty cases across the country, ones in which there was a white victim and an

African-American assailant, that race would become an issue in Hunt's execution.

We also knew that no matter *how* we addressed the matter of Jesse Jackson's visit, it would have to be done delicately. I was determined not to do anything that would impact the execution in a negative way. I didn't want the FOP—and by extension, the Baltimore Police Department—to become an issue.

The first thing I did was to contact people close to Parris Glendening. If the governor meets with the Rev. Jackson, I told them, he has to meet with Karen Adolfo and Vince's family, too. Fair is fair. Right is right.

I knew that would be a poison pill for Glendening and his staff. And I quickly received assurances that Jackson would not be granted an audience at the State House in Annapolis, and that the governor had no plans to stop Hunt's execution.

What we also had going for us was a very strong mayor, Kurt L. Schmoke. Schmoke had been the state's attorney when Vince Adolfo was killed; it was he who had made the decision to seek the death penalty for Hunt.

The Harvard-educated Schmoke was a tremendous ally of ours in this matter. "I have never had any doubts, any second thoughts about that case," he told reporters, miming a gun being fired with his thumb and forefinger to show how depraved he felt Hunt's actions were on that long ago day in Iron Alley.

The fact that Schmoke was a black man—the first African-American mayor elected into office in Baltimore—neutralized the incendiary issue of race that now loomed over Hunt's final days.

Those of us who wear the uniform always say that when

a bullet comes at a cop, it doesn't say black or white. If Vince had been an African-American, Hunt still would have shot him. And if Hunt had been white, Vince still would have chased him down that forlorn alley where he would breathe his last breath.

Still, Jesse Jackson's upcoming appearance in Charm City posed a problem for the FOP, especially from a PR point of view. Were we going to simply let him waltz into town and put on a show? Or do we somehow fight back on this narrative that the execution was all about race?

By this time, my phone was ringing off the hook with calls from enraged survivors—the term we used for family members of officers killed in the line of duty—and rank-and-file cops demanding that we respond to Jesse's visit.

A lot of my officers wanted to descend on the Supermax and protest. But after giving it a good deal of thought, I issued what was in effect a stand-down order. A protest would create an extremely volatile situation, and I didn't like the optics of our officers getting in shouting matches with any Jesse Jackson supporters.

So many of the cops eager to protest had been great friends of Vince. My God, many were still grieving his death! I could envision them gathering out front of the prison, holding signs and chanting, only to have some knucklehead from the other side say something stupid or provocative. Then suddenly there are bottles flying and punches being thrown and we have an ugly situation worsening by the minute.

No, I told my guys, I'll handle this.

I'll be there when Jesse Jackson shows up. And what we'll do is, we'll change the narrative being pushed by him and members of the Legislative Black Caucus. We're going to make it about Vince.

We're going to make it about the victim, not Flint Gregory Hunt. Because it's always the victim who gets left out of these things. The victim has no voice. And that's not just in *this* crime. It's in *any* crime.

So I hatched a plan.

The plan involved a silent protest of sorts. What I would do is make a sign that said simply: REMEMBER VINCE. And I would find a way to stand behind the Rev. Jackson when he addressed the media, as he inevitably would. And ideally I'd be positioned somewhere in the background, where the TV cameras had no choice but to record my presence, too.

The plan (he said modestly) worked to perfection.

When Jackson emerged from his half-hour meeting with Hunt and stepped up to the bank of microphones set up on the corner of Madison Street, I slid in behind him and held up my sign.

According to the Baltimore *Sun*, Jackson told reporters that most of his conversation with Hunt "was about the family of the dead policeman, about (Hunt's) sorrow, regret and pain… Not a day goes by that he does not think about this."

Jackson talked about leniency for Hunt and about the racial disparity on Death Rows all over the country. When he finished his brief remarks, he turned around and noticed me. This was my big moment. I introduced myself and we shook hands.

"Mr. Jackson," I said, "I just want everybody here to remember Vince Adolfo."

"Can we talk?" he asked.

"Sure," I said, and we walked down Madison Street and away from the media.

Our conversation was brief. I was struck by the reverend's quiet dignity and presence. He was cordial and seemed genuinely interested in what I had to say.

"Sir," I continued, "I just want you to know about Vince Adolfo. He was a really good cop. He made a difference in the community. He was loved by his entire family, including his young bride. And he didn't deserve what happened to him."

Jackson nodded gravely.

"I understand," he said. "I'm here because I don't want to see another black man killed."

"If Vince Adolfo were black," I said, "we'd still want the death penalty."

Neither one of us changed the other's mind about why we were there on that sun-scorched stretch of Madison Street. But I was pleased that he listened to me. I was glad I had a chance to tell him that Vince was not just another statistic, another nameless, faceless figure gunned down in the senseless violence that had consumed Baltimore seemingly forever.

I was even more happy—no, *ecstatic* is the better word—when I turned on the TV that night and saw that footage of me holding the "REMEMBER VINCE" sign behind the good reverend had made all the newscasts at 6 and 11. A big photo of the scene also appeared in the next day's *Sun*.

Yet that was to be the last pleasant memory many of us would have of that tumultuous 48 hours. Two days later, the Maryland Court of Appeals again stayed Hunt's execution, this time until at least September, when they would review the case again.

It was a gut punch. To ease the pain of it and to honor Vince and all the other fallen officers, we scheduled a prayer service later that day in front of police headquarters, timing it for 5 p.m. so it would receive maximum attention from the rush hour traffic whizzing by.

Jesse Jackson quickly issued a statement praising the Court of Appeals' decision. But in the next day's *Sun*, a photo appeared of a grief so palpable it took your breath away.

The photo showed Hilda Adolfo, Vince's mother, and his sisters Janet Grossnickle and Carol Miconi clutching each other, the three women shocked and despairing in the seconds after learning of this latest indignity to Vince's memory.

Karen Adolfo, Vince's young widow, was not pictured. Having heard the awful news, she had rushed to her husband's grave where, tearful and bereft, she had bowed her head and whispered: "I'm sorry."

19.

A Cop's Cop Gunned Down

The killing of Lt. Owen E. Sweeney Jr. and the incongruous circumstances surrounding it would haunt many of us in the Baltimore Police Department for years.

On the afternoon of May 7, 1997, Owen was at his desk in the Northeastern District, plowing through paperwork, when a call crackled over the radio. Officers had been summoned to a house on Bertram Avenue in Hamilton by a woman whose mentally-ill husband was refusing to take his medication and acting erratically.

Thinking he could be of help, Sweeney jumped in a patrol car and quickly joined his officers. This was not unusual on his part. Despite his rank, the 47-year-old Sweeney, with 28 years on the job, had always preferred being on the streets to the drudgery of desk work. A day earlier, in fact, he had report-edly been the first officer to confront a man attempting to rob a local shopping center with an Uzi semi-automatic.

Outside an apartment at the top of a second-floor stair-well, Sweeny attempted to talk to the agitated man standing behind a closed wooden door. "We're here to help you, not hurt you," Owen said, hoping to coax him out.

Officers had received assurances from the man's wife that there were no weapons inside the apartment. But when they turned to walk downstairs, they heard the man yell "Fuck you, pig!" Just then a blast from a 16-guage shotgun shattered the door, grievously wounding Owen in the lower back.

He stumbled and collapsed into the arms of Officer John D. Platt, a long-time friend and 14-year-veteran of the force. Platt and other officers pulled him down the stairs and out of the house. Moments later, the man who shot Owen, a 41-year-old named Baron Michael Cherry, walked out of the apartment with his hands up, apologizing for what he'd done and struggling with police as they took him into custody.

A distraught Denise Cherry, his wife, would later tell officers she'd forgotten about a shotgun her husband had received as a gift years earlier and kept in a bedroom closet. But this revelation came too late for Owen, who was flown by helicopter to Shock Trauma and into the operating room, clinging to life.

When I received the call about the shooting, I was stunned.

My first thoughts were: *Damn, it's a lieutenant! Lieutenants don't go on calls for service! A lieutenant shows up at a crime scene when all the bad shit's over with! Otherwise they're back at the station doing reports all day…*

As it happened, Owen and I had been neighbors in Bel Air. I didn't know him personally, but knew he lived about three blocks from me. And I was hopeful when I got to the hospital, because the word was that he was conscious, always a good sign.

Yet by the time Owen's wife, Elaine Sweeney, and their two sons, 25-year-old Owen III and 22-year-old Frank, arrived to join Owen's mom, dad, brother and sister in a grim vigil, the briefings from the doctors were growing increasingly dire.

Elaine had been whisked from her job at the Dundalk campus of Community College, Baltimore County and endured a harrowing ride to Shock Trauma in the back of a police car, with the siren wailing, lights flashing and the grim-faced lieutenant behind the wheel laying on the horn as they swerved through traffic.

Joined by the police chaplain in the room set up for the family, the Sweeneys hugged and prayed for a miracle. But a few hours later, on the third visit from the doctors, they received the heart-breaking news that Owen had died.

His death was a devastating blow to the department. It marked the first time a Baltimore police officer had been killed in the line of duty since 1992, when Ira Weiner had been gunned down in West Baltimore by a deranged crack addict.

It was also the first death of a cop on my watch as FOP president, and the first for Tom Frazier since he had taken over the police department. Yet when the commissioner showed up at the hospital, obviously shaken, as we all were, he proved to be an enormous comfort to Elaine and her family, offering heartfelt words of solace and seeing to their every need with food, beverages and transportation.

Frazier and I talked at the hospital, too. The usual built-in tensions between the union president and the police chief are always put aside during times of tragedy. And as the commish quietly told me about losing a good friend during his time in

San Jose, a motorcycle cop killed in a traffic accident, it did a great deal to humanize him in my eyes.

The line-of-duty death of *any* officer is always agonizing, of course. But there were tangential details about Owen's death that made it especially so.

Unbeknownst to many on the force, he was already making plans for his retirement. An inveterate fisherman and boater, he had just bought a 28-foot cabin cruiser to replace the more modest vessel he'd had for years.

The new boat was to be delivered within a week. And according to Elaine, Owen was literally counting down the days until its arrival, marking them off with growing excitement on a calendar each morning.

The manner of Owen's death, at the hands of a man diagnosed as a paranoid-schizophrenic, was also deeply unsettling.

"He was hearing voices, and (said) there were white worms crawling on his head," Denise Cherry would tell the *Sun* about her husband in a tearful interview two days later. Baron Michael Cherry had stopped taking his medication three weeks earlier, she claimed, and had grown increasingly angry and delusional since.

At the time, the police department had few guidelines for how its officers were to deal with a mental health crisis. (A detailed policy would not be released until June of 2021.)

Yes, the standoff would have been handled differently if police knew there was a weapon in the house. Tactical officers would have been called in to negotiate what likely would have become a barricade situation.

But a case could also be made that having a medical professional on hand, or having officers trained in strategies for de-escalating a crisis, might have helped defuse the situation enough to have Cherry surrender peacefully.

Not that any of that would have discouraged Owen Sweeney from rushing to the scene in the first place. He was a cop's cop, a supervisor who enjoyed working in the field and backing up his officers. And he had arrived at that apartment to help both his own men *and* Baron Cherry, as he said in his own words to the distraught man.

Over the years, I learned more and more about Owen and the life he led.

"He was rather quiet and shy and unassuming," Elaine told me. "He didn't need, nor did he seek, a lot of attention. He told me one time he could walk into a room filled with people, and if nobody acknowledged him, he'd be fine about it.

"And," she added, "he *loved* being a cop."

While Owen acknowledged the dangers inherent in his job, he, like most good police officers, never dwelled on them.

"I did all the worrying for both of us," Elaine said of her husband of 27 years. ". . . I worried more about him when he first went into the police department. Once he became a lieutenant, I thought he'd be OK."

She paused for a moment, then sighed. "I thought he was further removed from the dangers of the street."

The days that followed Owen's death were a painful and exhausting blur for the Sweeney family.

For the viewings at the Schimunek Funeral Home in Bel Air, the streets were choked with cars as hundreds of mourners gathered to pay their respects. (Among them, accompanying Commissioner Frazier, was Art Modell, the owner of the NFL Ravens, who would graciously invite Elaine and her sons to be his guests in his skybox at a game later that season.)

On the last night of the viewing, as the place was beginning to empty, Owen's dad approached me. With red-rimmed eyes and the agony of the past few days etched on his face, Owen Sr. had a favor to ask.

"I'd like to have my son's lieutenant's bars," he said softly.

The request startled me. It scared me a little bit, too. But there was no way I could turn him down. This was part of my job as the FOP president, to serve and comfort the families of these brave fallen officers—in any way possible.

Owen's casket was still open. I grabbed the funeral director and explained what we needed to do. Then I tracked down one of the police lieutenants lingering outside. And in short order, Owen's dad had the cherished keepsake he wanted, and a new set of lieutenant's bars were quietly pinned to the uniform of the hero now headed to his grave.

Owen's funeral would go on to be one of the largest police funerals in Maryland history. Along with dignitaries including Gov. Parris Glendening and Baltimore Mayor Kurt Schmoke, some 3,000 officers from 10 different states assembled at St. Margaret's Church for the funeral Mass, celebrated by Cardinal William H. Keeler, and the procession to Dulaney Valley Memorial Gardens in Timonium.

According to a story in the next day's *Sun*, the funeral cortege, consisting of 673 cars, was 18 miles long and took more than two hours to go the 30 miles from Bel Air to the burial site.

As it slowly moved southbound on I-95, we were treated to an amazing outpouring of tribute and support for Owen and his family.

All along the route, crowds could be seen on the overpasses, along with fire engines decked out with American flags and firefighters standing at attention and saluting. Little kids waved American flags; adults held signs saying "Thank you, Lt. Sweeney" and "God bless you, sir."

Elaine remembered seeing a man in a wheelchair along the route who struggled to his feet and placed his hat over his heart as the hearse went by.

All of these poignant gestures touched her and her family. Yet as the procession finally reached the cemetery, where the pageantry and tradition of a police farewell would be on full display, she couldn't help but imagine her husband gazing at the spectacle and thinking: *What's all the fuss about?*

"Owen was a very private person," she'd say years later. "He didn't want people to know a lot about his personal life. And how ironic that he died the way he did, and all of that became so public. His killing, his funeral, it was all so *public.*"

In a further touch of irony, as the wheels of justice ground slowly onward, it was Owen's killer who would disappear from public view altogether.

Baron Michael Cherry eventually pleaded guilty to shooting Owen Sweeney and was ordered confined to a maximum-security state hospital as part of a plea bargain, one that bewildered and infuriated Elaine Sweeney and her family, as well as the entire police department.

Four psychiatrists found Cherry competent to stand trial, but not legally responsible for the crime. The verdict, of course, amounted to even more layers of heartache and frustration for all who had known and loved Owen Sweeney.

"In my anger, I cannot help but wonder if this is really justice," Elaine said in the hushed courtroom that day, seeming to simultaneously address the presiding judge and her husband's murderer. "You have taken the life of our Owen and left us with so much pain, trauma and grief in exchange."

I was seething and despairing, too, especially for the half-dozen Sweeney family members on hand, and for every cop in Baltimore who would rightly view the ruling as a slap in the face.

"There is no guarantee that Mr. Cherry won't be walking the streets of Baltimore in six months, in five years or in 20 years," I told a *Sun* reporter when the hearing concluded. "There was no justice done here today."

20.

"This Man is Dead!"

It would be an additional year of torment for Vince Adolfo's family before another execution date was scheduled for Flint Gregory Hunt, this one for the week of June 30, 1997.

Once again, I was leery of getting my hopes too high and thinking that justice for the Adolfos was finally near. Yet there was also a sense that the endless appeals and stays granted Hunt might finally be coming to an end, and that his time on this earth was drawing to a close.

As the date drew near, William Sondervan would emerge as a central figure in the compelling drama of the state putting a condemned man to death.

Sondervan was a 22-year Army veteran, a career that had included a tour of duty in Vietnam as a combat engineer. Three years earlier, he had been tapped by Richard A. Lanham, the Commissioner of Correction, to be the assistant commissioner for security and operations of the vast Maryland prison system.

The new operations head was walking out the door after his initial meeting with his new boss when a bombshell—a figurative one this time—was dropped on him.

"Oh, by the way, we have an execution coming up," Lanham said casually. "I'm Catholic and it's all yours, buddy. I'm not going to do it."

With that, Sondervan returned to his office, put his head on his desk, and thought: *What the hell did I get myself into?*

Hunt had opted to die in the gas chamber, even though the choice of lethal injection was also open to him. Now it would be up to Sondervan to put together the execution team and plan the intricate details of a death by poison gas.

Resembling a diving bell, the hexagonal and forbidding-looking chamber had not been used in Maryland since 1961, when a rapist and murderer named Nathaniel Lipscomb was put to death.

"I had to kind of learn from scratch about the whole thing," Sondervan would recall years later. "The... execution was on my shoulders and I was scared to death. This was brand new territory for me."

One day, Sondervan visited Hunt in his cell, hoping to persuade him that dying by lethal injection was a far less grisly way to leave this world. This talk was not done for humanitarian reasons; the logistics involved in planning a gas chamber execution were infinitely more complicated for prison officials.

"Why do you want to get gassed?" Sondervan asked the prisoner. "Don't you know the gas chamber is a horrible experience and you're going to suffer?"

Patiently, Sondervan walked him through the entire deadly process, from the moment the condemned man entered the airtight space and was strapped into the chair, to the moment when the executioner pulled a lever that dropped the sodium cyanide pellets into a pool of sulfuric acid under the seat and the deadly cyanide gas began to waft upward.

"You're gonna get foamy at the mouth," Sondervan went on. "You're gonna have convulsions."

But Hunt was having none of it. After listening to this bleak tutorial, he stared balefully at Sondervan and replied: "I'm a Zulu warrior. And I want to make you motherfuckers pay for this."

Dutifully, Sondervan and his team prepared the gas chamber, located on the second floor of the Maryland Penitentiary's hospital wing, for Hunt's arrival. Except for training drills and tours, the chamber had not been used since 1961.

Now Sondervan and his men would begin rehearsing the steps involved in the execution process, including using chemical calibrators to test the levels of deadly gas.

But in case Hunt changed his mind, the team also traveled to Virginia to observe an execution by lethal injection, to see exactly how it was done and how it might affect them mentally and emotionally. Back in Baltimore, they held monthly sessions in which they practiced inserting IV lines into an anatomically-correct dummy; if the needle was inserted correctly in the vein, water would squirt out.

"I wasn't going to let anything go wrong with this execution," Sondervan told me. "Because everyone wanted a piece of your ass with this thing. A lot of people were hoping we'd screw it up."

Sondervan had a half-dozen different conversations with Hunt over the years, as the lengthy appeals process kept delaying his execution. When the death warrant was again handed down in June of 1997, Sondervan had another lengthy sit down with the condemned man, who was now was lashing out verbally at corrections officers and posing a physical threat, too.

"Hunt was a nasty SOB," Sondervan told me. "You knew if this guy ever caught you in an alley somewhere, he would rip your throat out and not even give it a second thought. He was a career criminal. This guy was just wired wrong. You could look in his eyes and tell that.

"He was kind of acting out at this point and the staff was worried [about how to deal with him.] So I… brought him to the Supermax and put him in this conference room, and I sat down with him. He was chained at the ankles, waist and wrists.

"I read him the death warrant," Sondervan continued. "When I got done, I set it down… and said 'Hunt, you got 30 days to live. And we can do this one of two ways. You can continue to be an asshole and I'm gonna treat you like an asshole. Or you can behave and be nice to my staff and be cooperative. And if you do that, I'll be as nice to you as I can possibly be."

Hunt looked at the older man and gulped. And within seconds, the simmering rage and contempt he'd shown toward his captors seemed to disappear. From that point on, there would be no more disciplinary issues involving Maryland's most infamous inmate.

In an interview with the *Sun* in the middle of June, Hunt continued to maintain that he wanted to die in the gas chamber. He'd heard jailhouse chatter about how peaceful the vicious murderer John Thanos had looked when put to death by lethal injection three years earlier. But Hunt wanted his own death to send a radically different message.

No, he said, he wanted the witnesses at his execution to see the full horror of the gas chamber, how ghastly and violent death in there could be

He insisted that the state was sanctioning his "murder." Therefore he wanted everyone to see him gasping and grunting and straining against his chest straps as he inhaled the deadly fumes, head whipping wildly back and forth, spittle flying from his mouth, torso shaking uncontrollably.

"My point is, I want people to have nightmares and dreams, and suffer like I suffer," he told a *Sun* reporter. "If it don't affect you [to bring about the execution], then it's like it don't affect me."

In a surprise move a week before he was to be executed, Hunt married a 34-year-old woman from Annapolis with whom he'd struck up a telephone relationship. The brief Muslim ceremony—he had converted to Islam in prison— took place in a room at the fortress-like Supermax, across from the Maryland Penitentiary.

A smattering of Hunt family members and stern-looking corrections officers were on hand, as guests and witnesses.

A Cinderella wedding, it was not.

"It was pretty quick," Sondervan recalled. "He was chained. She came into the room and they did the ceremony. He got to kiss her once, she was escorted out, and that was that."

That was not to be the last eye-opener orchestrated by Flint Gregory Hunt, however. Just days before the scheduled execution, he abruptly changed his mind about how he wanted to die.

Despite telling veteran WBAL-TV reporter Jayne Miller, in a phone interview, that he had "not accepted" the fact he'd soon be put to death for his crimes, he was now asking for a lethal injection over gas.

His lawyers would say the reason was simple: Hunt's new wife and mother wanted to witness the execution, and he was determined to spare the two women the sight of him writhing in agony in the gas chamber.

To the Adolfo family—and of course to me and my fellow FOP members—this was nothing but a naked ploy to delay his fate. But at an emergency court hearing to consider his request, his law team insisted it was "not a litigation tactic. We are not seeking a postponement of one minute… of his execution."

Initially, a city judge ruled it was too late to switch the method of execution. But the Maryland Court of Appeals quickly ruled in Hunt's favor, even though it was then decided his wife and mother would not be allowed to attend.

As the execution date approached, one of Sondervan's responsibilities was to see that a doctor was on hand to attend the execution and pronounce Hunt dead when it was over. Citing his Hippocratic oath, Dr. John E. Smialek, the chief medical examiner, said he would not come into the prison to issue the official death certificate until after the execution.

Through a friend in the corrections department of another state, Sondervan was able to hire a doctor, whom we will call "Dr. Smith" to do the job. A word of warning, the friend added: "This guy's a little strange."

"Strange," though, would turn out to be an understatement.

This became obvious in an initial telephone conversation Sondervan had with the good doctor, when he agreed, for a nominal fee, to come to Maryland for the execution. Sondervan then asked him if he had any special requirements for taking the job.

Yes, the doctor said. He wanted a corned beef sandwich. Oh, and a pickle, too.

On the night of the execution, however, it initially appeared "Dr. Smith" might not get to enjoy this sumptuous repast—not after he called prison officials to say he was lost somewhere on the Beltway.

The Maryland State Police were dispatched to find him and escort him to the prison. That was hardly the end of the weirdness, however. Because when he finally arrived, unkempt and with a long, scraggly beard, and went through the metal detectors, it was discovered the oddball physician was packing a handgun and a couple of fully-loaded clips.

Thankfully, these were surrendered without incident. But when he climbed the stairs to the second-floor death chamber and Sondervan introduced himself and stuck out his hand, "Dr. Jones" ignored the proffered mitt and said: "Where's my sandwich?"

Not until he finished eating it—and the pickle, of course— would the doctor talk to anyone.

"OK," he announced grandly, "I'm ready to go to work."

And so it was that a few minutes after midnight on July 2, with the 12 witnesses in place and Karen Adolfo and I huddled in the dim light next to them, separated only by a thin curtain, it was Bill Sondervan who went to the cell of the condemned man.

"Mr. Hunt," Sondervan said, "it's time to go."

"Sir," Hunt replied, "can I have one last prayer?"

When Sondervan agreed to the request, Hunt knelt on his prayer rug and recited a devotion in Arabic. He was then escorted, without shackles, into the death chamber, where he lifted himself onto the injection table, lay face up, and had an intravenous line inserted into each arm.

"I went over and talked to him one last time," Sondervan

remembered. "I asked him if he had anything he wanted to say."

But Hunt was through talking, seemingly exhausted and resigned to his fate. Three telephone lines had been set up in the room—one to the governor's office, one to the office of Maryland Attorney General Joseph Curran, and one to the U.S. Supreme Court—in case of a last-minute stay.

But the phones remained silent. Nothing was going to save Hunt on this day. Instead, another curtain, this one shrouding the death chamber, slid open.

As the execution began, Sondervan stood behind a partition off to one side, where the IV lines from Hunt were connected to a small box with three lights, indicating the order of the drugs to be administered.

On Sondervan's command, the first of the drugs, the sodium pentothal designed to render Hunt unconscious, flowed into the doomed prisoner's veins, after which he was heard to snore lightly.

The paralysis drug Pavulon came next, followed by the potassium chloride that would stop his heart from beating. And that was it. Hunt's eyes opened briefly, then closed for good. The curtain slid back into place.

After Karen and I left the room and the witnesses were escorted out, the peculiar doctor from out of town leaned over the body of Flint Gregory Hunt, listened for breathing and touched his carotid artery.

At 12:27 a.m., in a loud, theatrical voice, the doctor cried: "THIS MAN IS DEAD!"

The witnesses were taken downstairs to a conference room, where they talked to a psychologist about what they had just seen. When that session ended, Sondervan and his execution team, as well as the officers who had been on the death watch outside Hunt's cell for many months, were debriefed by the same psychologist.

He explained some of the likely emotions the men might be feeling, based on volumes of research done on those who had overseen executions in the past. Then he gave out his phone number and urged them to call with any issues they might have going forward.

In the following weeks and months, some team members would end up calling for help, plagued with problems such as sleeping and eating disorders.

Significantly, one who didn't call was Bill Sondervan.

It was a decision he would go on to regret

"{The execution} was hard on everyone," he told me later. "Hunt was an animal. But you still took the life of a human being. Every single person on that team still feels it to the core. It actually bothered me a lot."

Sondervan had suffered from PTSD after being plunged into the Vietnam War as an 18-year-old in 1968. He'd spent a year on dangerous missions with infantry and armored units as he and his buddies built roads and bridges while braving sniper fire, negotiating roads and fields strewn with land mines and seeing countless vehicles blown up.

Now, the execution of Flint Gregory Hunt would bring on another bout of PTSD.

"This thing with Hunt, when we were going through it, I was so focused and so scared and so stressed," he said. "When it was all over, it kind of kicked in some nightmares with me. It was tough for me for a while.

"I should have talked to a shrink."

21.

"10-50 Red!"

Police officers confront the fragility of life and their own mortality on a daily basis—this is no great revelation. But in the fall of 1998, the BPD suffered another pair of back-to-back tragedies that seemed almost incomprehensible, even to the most hardened veterans of the force.

The first was the death of Officer Harold J. Carey, killed when the police van he was riding in collided with a police cruiser at an intersection as both raced to assist a fellow officer. Just a few days later, even as hundreds of officers in their dress blue uniforms mourned at Carey's funeral, another disaster was unfolding near the B&O Railroad Museum on West Pratt Street.

Along with my FOP vice-president Brian May, I was leaving the service for Carey and heading to the cemetery when the terse message "10-50 Red! 10-50 Red!" crackled over the radio. It chilled us both.

It meant that Foxtrot, the police helicopter, was going

down. The pilot, Flight Officer Barry Wood, was signaling that the chopper had lost power. A catastrophic engine failure had occurred.

We pulled out of the funeral procession and raced to the crash site. The next radio dispatch was equally ominous: police were already clearing a route to Shock Trauma for the ambulances that would transport Barry and his aerial observer, Officer Mark Keller.

At the hospital, we learned the grisly details of what had happened. Wood, a veteran of 27 years on the force who had flown helicopters for the Army in the Vietnam War, had been flying at a fairly low altitude as he and Keller, a 21-year veteran, chased a stolen car.

But as they circled the streets above Southwest Baltimore, smoke began pouring from the tiny, two-seat chopper.

It quickly lost altitude and crashed to the ground, smashing into an iron fence near the museum entrance and bursting into flames. The officers who had been chasing the stolen car pulled off their pursuit and raced to the crash scene, pulling both men from the wreckage.

Both had suffered severe injuries, but Woods' were thought to be far worse. The chopper had landed on its left side, which meant the pilot had taken the brunt of the impact. And while Keller had been pulled from the fiery mass of twisted metal fairly quickly, Barry had been trapped for several minutes until firefighters managed to free him.

At a little after 3 p.m., when I ran into Dr. Thomas Scalea and asked about Wood's condition, the famed chief trauma surgeon said simply: "It's real bad, Gary." Two hours later, after having been rushed into surgery, Barry died of heart failure.

Mark Keller, we learned, had emerged from the crash with

a broken elbow and spinal fracture.

(At Barry's funeral a week later, Mark would acknowledge Barry's heroics, how he had tilted the chopper on the pilot's side just before impact to give his partner a chance to survive. "There is no greater love than this: to lay down one's life for one's friends," Keller said, quoting from the Gospel of St. John.

("Barry did that for me," Keller went on. "Because of that, I will always love him, and my family will always love him, all the days of our lives.")

As Shock Trauma began filling with family, friends and shaken cops, along with Mayor Kurt Schmoke and Commissioner Tom Frazier, Brian May and I began the work we (unfortunately) knew so well by now: setting up areas where the families could congregate privately, arranging for food deliveries, making hotel arrangements for relatives coming in from out-of-town.

Martha Wood, Barry' wife of 28 years, was already at the hospital. But we arranged for a state police plane to pick up other members of Barry's family in West Virginia and fly them to Martin State Airport in Middle River, where we'd have cars to ferry them to the hospital.

Even though we were still in the early hours of this latest tragedy, there was already speculation about how the crash would affect the operations of the Foxtrot fleet.

The truth was, despite the all-important important role they played, helicopter pilots like Barry Wood were fairly anonymous members of the police force. The street cops really didn't get to know them. The pilots drove out to Martin State every day, went up in the air, did their jobs, came down and went home.

They didn't really mix with other cops. They didn't even communicate with us on the radio. That was the observer's job --the pilot was too damn busy flying the chopper for any conversation, idle or otherwise.

Nevertheless, the officers on the ground viewed the pilots with unabashed awe and admiration. Most of the ones hired by the BPD back then had, like Barry, piloted choppers in combat operations in Vietnam.

No wonder they radiated an eerie calm as they patrolled the skies above a perilous city. Let's face it, when you've spent a few years ferrying troops into battle and rescuing injured soldiers while dodging rocket and machine gun fire, you're unlikely to be fazed by some knucklehead from West Baltimore who just robbed a convenience store and is now on the run.

These pilots of ours were the best of the best. They were the ones who watched over the rest of us, a reassuring presence on high for the men and women in blue doing their own dangerous work on the streets below.

Imagine this scenario: you're a patrol officer. It's the middle of the night when you get a call to investigate a possible break-in at a warehouse. You get there and the place is as dark as a cave. Your puny department-issued three-cell flashlight does not exactly cast a wide beam, making it maybe just a notch or two above useless.

Now as you go around looking under cars and checking windows and jiggling doorknobs, you're so on edge you can feel your heart thumping, like it'll burst through your chest at any moment.

Yet suddenly you hear Foxtrot overhead.

In the next instant, a spotlight lights the place up like it's daytime. Almost immediately you begin to calm down. Now you know no one's sneaking up on you. No one's grabbing you from behind. No one's pulling out a gun and waiting for you around the next corner, or in that nearby alley.

Foxtrot has your back from 500 feet up in the air. Or 1,000 feet up. Or whatever the case may be.

When I was huffing and puffing and chasing that little turd across the Morgan State campus all those years ago and Foxtrot appeared out of nowhere, I nearly wept with gratitude. Hell, I wanted to blow kisses to those guys.

Helicopters are such a force-multiplier for the police. And the bad guys know it. How many criminals have surrendered the minute they spotted Foxtrot overhead? The list is endless. When Foxtrot got on you, believe me, you were *not* getting away.

Think about it: if you were some mope on the lam and you tried running into a house, Foxtrot was high enough in the sky that it could cover the front and back entrances. And if you stayed put, if you didn't do something stupid like try to bolt out a side window, Foxtrot could wait you out until reinforcements arrived and they dragged you away in handcuffs.

Yet now, in the immediate aftermath of the horrific crash that killed Barry Wood and nearly cost Mark Keller his life, the future of the Foxtrot fleet was in doubt.

Sure enough, the remaining three choppers were quickly grounded. Investigators began trying to determine the cause of the disastrous engine failure that caused Wood's aircraft to spiral out of the heavens.

The fleet would not fly again until 2001, when money was raised to bring a whole new unit back. And this time, the city would have its own employees maintaining the helicopters, not an outside contractor.

During those intervening years, though, Foxtrot was keenly missed by the cops on the streets, now doing their hazardous jobs without an eye in the sky to watch over them.

22.

Not Bad For A Kid From Waverly

It was early November of 1998 when the national president of the FOP called with what seemed a bizarre question.

"How would you like to speak at the White House with the president?" Gil Gallegos asked.

What?! Was this another practical joke? By now I was starting to feel like the home office for every dumb cop prank in the book. *Sure, let's tell McLhinney the prez wants to see him! Hell, who's more gullible than Gary?!*

But it turned out Gil was dead serious. President Bill Clinton was about to sign two new bills, addendums to the historic 1994 Violent Crime Control and Law Enforcement Act, generally referred to as the Crime Bill. And I was being asked to deliver some remarks at the ceremony, which would actually take place at the Old Executive Office Building, next door to the White House.

Full disclosure: I was not exactly a Democratic supporter of the president. But I was definitely a supporter of the Crime Bill and all that came with it. I also knew the president was a staunch advocate for this country's law enforcement agencies, and had been for years.

Now he was about to sign into law two important bills that were near and dear to my heart. One would provide educational assistance to the dependents of local and state officers killed or permanently injured in the line of duty, expanding on an existing federal program. The other closed a loophole regarding gun crimes, imposing longer sentences on criminals who used guns in crimes of violence or drug trafficking.

The truth was, my being asked to speak at the signing didn't actually come out of left field, either. For one thing, I was on the national FOP board of directors, the youngest ever elected at age 30. Also, because we were so close to D.C., the Baltimore Police Department would often provide uniformed officers to serve as backdrops for various presidential photo ops.

But this was going to involve far more than just standing behind the Commander-in-Chief with a frozen grin while he speechified, then getting a quick handshake when it was over. This would involve actual preparation, the hard work of committing cogent thoughts to paper in order to avoid looking like a sweating, stammering fool in front of a VIP audience and a ton of reporters.

Yet right away, I said yes to Gallegos. Then as soon as I hung up, I thought: *Holy shit, what did I just DO?*

As I found out, you can't just show up at a presidential bill signing and start blabbing whatever you want. Everything has to be approved. So I ended up working with both the White

House staff and the national FOP to craft my remarks.

A few days later, I dusted off a clean dress uniform, jumped in my car and headed down to Washington.

I had been asked to bring along a "survivor" of a police shooting, so it was only natural that I chose Kim Deachilla. Kim was the widow of Officer Billy Martin, who had been shot and killed 10 years earlier, ambushed in a stairwell when he responded to a complaint of drug dealing at a West Baltimore apartment building.

Kim is an extraordinary woman. In the years since Billy's death, she had channeled her shock and grief into raising their son Patrick, who was only 3 when his father was murdered. (Patrick, with her blessing, would go on to become a Baltimore police officer and wear his father's shield.) She had also remarried, raised a daughter and worked for the FOP as my assistant, doing key PR and strategic planning and offering advice and comfort to the wives of other fallen officers.

Somehow, leaning heavily on her Catholic faith, she had also found a way to forgive Billy's killer, a man named Shawn Woodson, who was 20 at the time of the murder and who remains in prison to this day after his death sentence was overturned by the Maryland Court of Appeals.

Joining us on the car ride to D.C. was my old partner from my vice work days, Charmaine Thomas, who'd apparently exonerated me for that stunt we pulled on her with the geezer john at the Marylander motel. Bob Richards, an African-American cop in charge of a committee I'd established to address the concerns of minority officers, was the fourth member of our traveling party.

We spent the ride laughing and joking and marveling over our good fortune, at how cool it would be to participate in such an important event in such an august setting. I wasn't nervous at this point. Not until we arrived at the Old Executive Office Building and they separated us—Kim was to be in the audience, Charmaine and Bob would be part of the backdrop for the ceremony—did the jitters start to kick in.

I was escorted to a separate room, where a stone-faced Secret Service agent asked me if I wanted something to drink. When I gestured to some water bottles on a nearby table, he pointedly explained that they were not for me. Instead of shooting me right then and there for being a hopeless rube, however, he was kind enough to retrieve a bottle of water from a nearby closet.

One of the president's aides came in, asked how I pronounced my name, and then practiced intoning it into a nearby microphone. After that, Sandra Grace, a police officer from Massachusetts and the head of the National Organization of Police Officers, joined us; she was to be another speaker on the program.

It was at this point that the door suddenly opened again. And into the room, with zero fanfare or entourage, strolled the President of the United States.

Well. If I was a little anxious beforehand, the butterflies were now doing strafing runs in my stomach. Flashing a genial smile, Bill Clinton greeted me with a hearty "Detective McLhinney," shook my hand and pulled me closer.

OK, I confess: I was in total awe.

The president was taller than I'd expected, with an incredibly commanding presence. Yet he also seemed genuine and approachable. Pundits have noted that Clinton may have the most superb eye contact of any politician in recent memory. No wonder people who met him tended to say the same thing:

when he looked at you, you felt as if you were the only person in the room.

"How are things in Baltimore?" he asked, as we made small talk.

I checked the impulse to unload on him about the latest catastrophes befalling my hometown, from the rising crime rate, worsening drug-dealing and the rest of the social ills. Instead, all I said was: "My guys are working really hard, sir. It's a tough city."

"I know they are," the president replied. "And we appreciate it."

Did I mention he was still embroiled at this point in the Monica Lewinsky sex scandal, the one that had riveted the nation? And that just three months earlier, he had gone on live TV to admit to an inappropriate relationship with the then-22-year-old White House intern? And that he'd recently been impeached in the House of Representative on one count of perjury and another for obstruction of justice?

I should probably mention that. Because given his relaxed and cheerful demeanor, you would have thought that the Bill Clinton standing before me, despite the awesome demands of his office and the howling jackals of the media on his heels, had not a care in the world.

Talk about someone who could compartmentalize! In addition, Mr. Clinton was dealing with a growing crisis with Iraq, which was thought to be developing weapons of mass destruction and refusing to cooperate with United Nations weapons inspectors.

Again, you would have never known any of this was on the president's mind as he chatted up Officer Grace and me.

Soon it was time for the ceremony to begin. As we filed

out into the ornate chamber where it would be held, a boom-
ing voice over the loudspeaker announced: "LADIES AND
GENTLEMEN, THE PRESIDENT OF THE UNITED
STATES, ACCOMPANIED BY DETECTIVE GARY
MCLHINNEY AND ---."

To be honest, much of what followed was a blur. My
nerves were kicking in big-time at this point.

As we took the stage, with a dozen or so police officers
solemnly providing the background, I spotted a number of
political big-shots: Attorney General Janet Reno; Joe Biden,
then the Democratic Senator from Delaware; Bart Stupak,
the Democratic congressman from Michigan; Peter King, the
Republican congressman from New York. (The two new laws
had been passed by Congress on a bi-partisan basis. Imagine
that in this day and age!)

In addition to the 40 or so dignitaries in the audience,
there was a huge press contingent on hand, with some three
dozen TV cameras pointing at us from risers in the back of the
room and live coverage on C-SPAN.

I was a veteran of news conferences, having participated
in many through my work with the FOP. But I'd never seen
a media presence like this, much of it driven, of course, by
the misconduct in the Oval Office with Lewinsky and the
saber-rattling over Iraq.

Congressman Stupak kicked off the program with brief
remarks about the two bills. He was followed by Congressman
King and Senator Biden, who also extolled the virtues of the
new legislation.

It was while Biden was speaking that President Clinton
leaned over to me and, looking at the audience, whispered:
"Hey, who's that guy in the front row?"

I whispered back that the distinguished-looking gentleman in question was none other than J. Joseph Curran Jr., Maryland's Attorney General. Not for nothing, though, was the president considered one of the most talented politicians of his era, with an astounding memory for names and faces. Right then and there, I was willing to bet that never again would he gaze on the ruddy visage of Joe Curran and not know who he was.

It was after Biden spoke—he concluded with "Mr. President, you are the best friend cops *ever* had in the White House"—that the program went, um, slightly *awry*.

I had been told I would be the next speaker, and that Biden would introduce me. Instead, when he finished, the veteran lawmaker from the First State promptly folded his printed remarks, turned on his heel and... sat down.

There followed an awkward few seconds in which everyone looked around as if thinking: *OK, what's next?* Only then did Biden hustle back to the podium with a sheepish look on his face.

"I got so carried away, I forgot to introduce a cop!" he said. "They wondered, as an Irishman, whether I'd be able to pronounce his name. His name is McLhinney! I had no problem with that."

A ripple of laughter could be heard. That was all Biden needed.

"I just had a granddaughter, Mr. President," he continued. "And... her first name is Finnegan. She better turn out to be beautiful and smart. But there's no doubt she's Irish."

This got even more laughs. Joe Biden was on a roll!

As has been well-chronicled, there have been many occasions throughout his political career when Biden's staff has had to practically drag him away from the microphone after his allotted time was up.

Mercifully, this was not one of them.

Turning to me, he said: "Detective, come on up here, since I blew your opening, and tell them what's going on."

As introductions go, it wasn't the most eloquent ever accorded me. I managed to grin and shake the senator's hand. But by the time I reached the podium, I was a world-class nervous wreck. You can still catch my remarks on C-SPAN's archives, if you're ever so inclined. And if you are, you will see the most mournful-looking man ever to step up to a microphone.

I looked like my dog had just been run over.

A minute or so into my remarks, my anxiety seemed to ratchet up another notch when my right leg began shaking. Shaking uncontrollably, too. So now I was thinking: *Can people see this?!* The president was seated slightly behind me and to my right. I didn't think there was any way in hell he could miss it. Nor, probably, could the cops arrayed behind us, who had to be ready to bust a gut laughing at my obvious discomfort.

Of course, fixating on the fact that your leg is now vibrating like a ceiling fan is not exactly conducive to delivering a crisp and effective speech. It felt like I was about to fall over. But somehow I put my head down and finished my remarks, the gist of which expressed my gratitude to the president, on behalf of the 277,000 members of the FOP, for supporting the new bills and getting them passed through Congress.

I might have been nervous, but I meant every word of it.

After Officer Grace spoke and the president delivered the keynote address, assuring that America was now safer and that the families of slain officers had been helped immensely, some of us stood behind the president as he signed the legislation into law.

It was an emotional moment. When he was through, the president handed out the pens he had used on the documents. All these years later, I still have mine squirreled away somewhere. It's a memento I'll always cherish.

On the ride back to Baltimore, as we dissected the day's happenings, Kim, Charmaine and Bob wanted to know what the president had whispered to me during Joe Biden's speech.

"He was asking for dating advice," I replied. I thought it was a pretty good line. It played well in the car, anyway.

All of us, I think, were happy to have been part of such an important occasion, yet relieved that it was over, too. As for me, I also felt a tremendous sense of accomplishment that measures I'd long advocated for would finally come into being, and that my remarks had been well-received. (Apparently, I'd done a better job than I thought camouflaging my nerves.)

Over the course of my life, whenever certain positive events had occurred, I'd often say to myself: "Not bad for a kid from Waverly."

I was definitely saying it again now.

23.

A Political Rock Star Emerges

In the spring of 1999, Baltimore was embroiled in a contentious mayoral campaign in which issues of race, class and nepotism, which had simmered quietly in the background, burst into view.

And guess who was in the middle of it all?

That's right: your friendly neighborhood FOP president, convinced that my beloved organization could only benefit—in terms of pay, pensions and overall support—with an expanded role in city politics.

Charm City was in a sour mood back then. Crime was up, the murder rate seemed intractable, schools were failing, neighborhoods were in serious decline. To no one's surprise, Baltimore continued to hemorrhage residents, losing 14 percent of its population in the previous decade.

Kurt L. Schmoke, the city's first elected African-American

mayor, had declined to run for a fourth term. This kicked off a veritable parade of candidates—some legitimate, others outright pretenders—practically elbowing each other to replace him.

To no one's surprise, the FOP was excited about this election.

Now there existed the real possibility that the police department would also be getting new leadership. Crime was the top issue in the campaign and Tom Frazier, the present police commissioner, was widely disliked by both the rank-and-file and the leading candidates to replace Schmoke,

Frazier's faults as a commissioner were many and obvious to all.

He didn't have a clue how to motivate street cops or detectives to run down alleys and crash through doors to get the bad guys. He never articulated a crime plan or strategy to stem the growing violence in the city.

He was never seen on the street with the cops, except for photo ops at ribbon cuttings and Police Athletic League center openings. His mortal sin of rotating officers out of specialized units was never forgiven. And he proudly called himself a social worker with a gun, a term most police officers hated.

We weren't hired to be social workers. Our job was to enforce the laws.

Little wonder, then, that we saw the mayoral race as a once-in-a-lifetime opportunity to influence the outcome and get our guy elected to dump Frazier. And our guy was Lawrence Bell III, the 37-year-old president of the City Council and a staunch supporter of law enforcement. All the city unions—police, firefighters, City Union of Baltimore (the bargaining agent for municipal workers) and AFSCME—had coalesced around him as the Democratic primary neared.

Although he had yet to announce his candidacy, he was the clear front-runner in most polls. It gave the FOP, often seen as a bunch of white cops, the opportunity to support an African-American candidate. We also hoped to see Martin O'Malley, the 36-year-old Northeast Baltimore councilman and Bell's pal, ascend to the City Council presidency.

O'Malley, a lawyer and reform-minded populist who also fronted an Irish rock band called "O'Malley's March," was another strong supporter of police. He had been our work-horse on the City Council, involved in all our pension legislation and chair of the Finance Committee, and he and I had become friends.

Teaming up four years earlier, Bell and O'Malley had fashioned themselves as courageous outsiders willing to take on what they saw as an appalling lack of leadership from the Schmoke administration. Nicknamed "Batman and Robin," the two became known for their criticism of the feckless crime-fighting strategies of Schmoke and Frazier, and for demanding accelerated progress in making Baltimore safer.

Little wonder, then, that the pair was perceived as a dream ticket for cops. At a meeting at the FOP hall, our membership voted overwhelmingly to support Bell. I held off a vote for City Council president only because O'Malley had not yet announced his intention to run. Yet we were certain that was only a matter of time.

In fact, we were so certain that we held a big fund-raiser at the FOP hall for Martin. He played with his band and they packed the place. Back then he was fond of saying that traditional Irish music could sound like someone banging a cat against a wall. But O'Malley's March could *rock*. Even their rebel tunes that veered into more standard kill-the-Brits territory brought down the house.

As the primary neared, however, we started to hear rumors of tension between the two old friends. In the beginning of June, a headline in the *Sun* blared: "Bell-O'Malley bond appears to weaken; city councilmen deny recent differences are signs of a rift."

We were also hearing that Schmoke allies, like the influential political consultant Julius Henson and George Balog, the powerful Director of Public Works, were lining up for Bell. (Balog, was known as "The Boss" for his iron-fisted control of 6,000 employees and an annual budget of a whopping $500 million.)

And that faction was supposedly whispering in his ear: *Lawrence*, you *gotta steer clear of Martin. You're being seen as his lapdog. It's like Martin's pulling your strings. You don't need the white guy to win this race.*

On the heels of that came scuttlebutt that O'Malley, too, was planning to run for mayor. Since we were backing Bell and still hoped to have Martin lead the City Council, the city's unions asked me to sit down with the two, explain what we wanted, and try to work out any friction between them.

I decided to take them for lunch at Chiapparelli's, the popular eatery in Little Italy. Who doesn't like great Italian food, right? Who doesn't like a delicious order of Drooling Gnocchi or Mama's Ravioli, with a fine glass of Chianti or Lambrusco to go with it?

Oh, yeah, I thought, *we'll work things out. It'll be a nice, relaxing meal.*

Except… it turned out to be as relaxing as a knife fight.

On the day of the lunch, I picked up Martin at City Hall.

He was in a pensive mood. He talked about spending an inordinate time on his Council duties, a job that paid very little. He also hinted that his law practice was struggling.

"I gotta either make some money or I'm gonna remain a poor councilman," he told me as we drove.

When we got to Chiapparelli's, Lawrence was already there. In a surprise move, he had also brought along his brother Marshall as his *consigliere.* Both were sitting on the same side of the table, which I found odd.

A tacit sign that battle lines were being drawn?

It definitely looked that way.

The tension was palpable from the onset. There was no light-hearted banter as we nibbled on bread and placed our orders. What little small talk there was seemed strained, punctuated by uncomfortable silences.

Sensing that this little summit could blow up in a hurry, I plowed ahead with what the city's unions wanted to see: a ticket of Lawrence as mayor and Martin as City Council head, with incumbent Joan Pratt as Comptroller.

This did not exactly elicit high-fives all around.

"I don't want to make a commitment until after the filing deadline," Lawrence declared flatly.

Marshall quickly chimed in. Looking pointedly at Martin, he said: "We don't see that you'd bring anything to the ticket."

Well.

I thought Martin was going to come across the table at him. *I* wanted to come across the table at him. From then on, Martin ignored Marshall, directing all his remarks exclusively to Lawrence.

"You're being controlled by these guys," he said of the Schmoke partisans, whom he referred to as "old warhorses."

"This isn't you."

Moments later, when Lawrence asked directly if Martin planned to run for mayor, O'Malley hesitated.

"Well," he said finally, "my sense is that you're dropping like a rock."

Our nice, relaxed meal went straight downhill from there.

It devolved into charges of betrayal and negativity being hurled back and forth. And it ended with O'Malley saying he was still unsure about what office he'd seek, and Lawrence saying he'd *think* about a ticket with Martin on it.

There was no: "Hey, let's see what the polls look like" between the two." No: "Hey, I love you, you and I came into the Council together, we're a team, let's work this out."

Instead, the handwriting was on the wall, scrawled in neon letters 10 feet high: a Bell-O'Malley ticket was doomed.

When I dropped Martin off at City Hall, we sat in silence for a moment.

Finally, I said: "You know we already endorsed him…"

"I know," he said.

"This is really gonna be fucked up if we can't get this worked out," I added.

With a half-smile, Martin said: "I understand what you guys did."

Ruminating on it later, I thought it was Martin's way of telling me: *If I run for mayor, I know why the unions did what they did in endorsing Lawrence.*

In late May, Bell officially declared his candidacy for the office. Noticeably absent for the occasion was Martin, citing a prior commitment in court with a client. And sure enough, on June 22, O'Malley announced his own bid to become the 47th mayor of Baltimore.

Like many in our FOP membership, I thought Martin had a snowball's chance in hell of winning. A white guy in a majority black city? In *this* majority black city? No way.

This was no longer the Baltimore of the last white guy to hold that office, the fiery William Donald Schaefer, who held it for four terms until his election as governor in 1987. The city had changed. The racial fault lines had widened dramatically.

Former City Councilman Carl Stokes, another African-American candidate for mayor, was gaining support from certain religious groups and key lawmakers in both East Baltimore and West Baltimore. But even if Martin were somehow able to split the Bell-Stokes votes, I didn't see how he could prevail.

Yet others closer to him, it seemed, were far more optimistic.

Two days after Martin declared his candidacy, I was sitting at a red light at the corner of President and Lombard streets when I noticed a car in front of me covered with O'Malley for Mayor stickers.

Suddenly, the driver got out and walked back to my car. It was Katie O'Malley, Martin's wife.

"When we win this election," she said sweetly, "you're gonna have to kiss this First Lady's ass."

I didn't really take this as a threat; Katie was smiling. Plus I had known her and her family for years. But I can't say it didn't make me a *little* nervous. Politics is a blood sport, after all. And I had just taken a stiff jab to the nose, albeit with a velvet glove.

Even though the city's unions doubled-down on their support of Lawrence Bell and his wealthy backers continued to pour money into his coffers, his campaign soon turned into a dumpster fire.

Financial troubles dogged him. The media played up the fact that he'd been sued three times for failing to pay personal debts. His car had also been repossessed. And a damaging story emerged about Lawrence going to New York and using campaign funds to buy bespoke suits. (Columnist Dan Rodricks of the *Sun* labeled it "a $4,000 campaign shopping spree at Sak's Fifth Avenue.")

There was more: a group of Bell's backers, led by Julius Henson, were roundly criticized for shouting down speakers at an O'Malley rally. And Bell workers were found to have distributed racist flyers in African-American neighborhoods, and attributing them to the O'Malley campaign.

Carl Stokes' chances to win also took a hit when it was discovered that his campaign flyers stated that he'd graduated from Loyola College. It turned out he had attended the school, but never earned a diploma.

By September, O'Malley's words seemed prescient: Bell's poll numbers were sinking precipitously. When the election finally rolled around, Martin won the Democratic primary handily, with 53 percent of the vote. ("White Man Gets Mayoral Nomination in Baltimore," read the headline in *The Washington Post*.)

Even though he would now face Republican developer David Tufaro in the general election, in this overwhelmingly Democratic city, a win in the primary was tantamount to already being elected. For the record, Stokes finished second in the primary with 28 percent of the vote. Bell collected just 17 percent.

On Election Night, after visiting the morgue that was Bell campaign headquarters, a number of us repaired to the FOP hall in Hampden to ease our disappointment with alcohol. We consoled ourselves with the thought that our nemesis,

Commissioner Tom Frazier, would soon be gone. In fact, Martin had used that exact word, "gone," when asked, immediately after his win, about Frazier's future.

Yet after all the work we'd put in to see Lawrence elected, it was still a pretty tough night. I called Martin to congratulate him, and to tell him the FOP was obviously prepared to work with him to achieve our long-standing goal of making Baltimore safer.

Then I had a brainstorm (he again said modestly.) I invited him to the next FOP meeting.

Again, he packed the place. Normally I'd get 75 to 80 members at these meetings. For this one, it was standing room only. We stopped counting the crowd at 800, even though it was fire-marshal-approved for no more than 300.

"The Tom Frazier era is over," I said when introducing the de-facto next mayor. "We're with you. You lead and we'll follow."

Martin gave a lengthy speech expounding on his vision of the policing the city so desperately needed. He was articulate and thoughtful throughout. And when he finished, he received a standing ovation from an audience of weary, embattled and jaded cops that he'd somehow found a way to energize.

He also announced that I would be a member of his transition team focused on crime, something we'd discussed earlier and something that had never been done before.

I was pleased to hear this, of course. Yet standing there with the lanky, charismatic Irishman, what I felt, too, was a renewed sense of hope for the entire police department.

Martin O'Malley was an emerging political rock star. You had to be blind not to see that after his long-shot victory. He was laser-focused on making the city safer. And that could only make life easier for my brothers and sisters in blue.

24.

A Shake-up In The War On Crime

To no one's surprise, Police Commissioner Tom Frazier did not stick around for his official sacking.

Not long after the primary elections, Frazier, no dummy, lit out for a new job with the U.S. Justice Department. Somewhat delusional to the end, the man brought in five years earlier to reform the police department told reporters he felt he had achieved his goals of reducing crime and restoring confidence in the force.

We in the FOP politely refrained from laughing in public over these statements. Privately, however, they kept us in stitches for days.

As expected, Martin O'Malley cruised to victory in the general election, largely on the strength of his promise to stem the city's burgeoning murder rate and close down open-air drug markets.

Martin was calling for an aggressive "zero tolerance" strategy to fight crime, modeled after the one used in New York City by Mayor Rudy Giuliani. It involved arresting people for minor offenses like loitering, public drinking and public urination, with the goal of catching fugitives, maintaining order and curtailing more serious offenses.

To be sure, not everyone was on board with this strategy. A number of African-American civic and religious leaders feared it would lead to undue police harassment of black citizens. But that didn't seem to deter Martin. Nor did the criticism he received for hiring Jack Maple, a former New York police consultant with a national reputation for inventive master plans that had helped reduce crime in cities like New Orleans and Newark, N.J.

(This outside expertise did not come cheap; Maple and his partner, John Linder, were being paid a cool $2,000 a day.)

Yet in late December of 1999, when Martin announced the hiring of Ron Daniel as his new police commissioner, it seemed to soften many of the misgivings city leaders had about "zero tolerance."

Daniels, 50, an African-American and 26-year-veteran of the police department, was highly-respected by the rank-and-file and lauded for his honest, hard-working, no-bullshit style of management.

"Colonel Daniel is the kind of strong leader we're looking for," I told reporters.

Equally important: Daniel knew the city. He was one of us; rightly promoted from within. We had just come off five-plus years with an outsider from the West Coast running the department. The last thing we needed was another outsider telling us, the once-proud *POH-LEECE* of Baltimore, how we were screwing up.

Daniel, it was thought, would get us back on track.

On the other hand, I wasn't surprised when Martin quickly tapped Edward T. Norris, deputy commissioner of operations for the New York Police Department, to be the assistant commissioner. I knew Martin was impressed with the NYPD's operations and the dramatic bite they had taken out of crime. Murders, for one thing, had been reduced from 2,000 in 1993 to fewer than 700 within five years.

He was equally impressed with CompStat, a computerized method for tracking crime—complaints, arrests and summons activity—instituted in all of the 77 New York police precincts. And now that Jack Maple was on board, the hiring of another ambitious cop from the Big Apple to be Daniel's operations guy didn't seem so strange.

As part of O'Malley's transition team, and at the behest of Daniel, I met with Ed Norris at the Paper Moon diner in Hampden not long after he was hired. Right away I could tell he was a brash, ambitious, no-nonsense guy, totally energized and determined to make his mark by cleaning up the murder and heroin capital of the country.

All of us knew this one certainty: if you could make a dent in crime in Baltimore, you could write your ticket to any chief's job in all 50 states. I also knew the troops would love him. *They'll bust their asses for this guy,* I thought. *Martin made two great hires here. Daniel and Norris will make a helluva team.*

Unfortunately, the relationship between Martin and Daniel deteriorated quickly. And once again, I seemed to be in the middle of it all.

The FOP was gearing up for contract negotiations with the new mayor, focused on pay, benefits and working conditions, when we began to hear of bickering between O'Malley and Daniel.

The new commissioner was said to be feeling left out as O'Malley's high-priced, out-of-town consultants went about implementing the city's crime-fighting plan. The new mayor, on the other hand, was reported to be frustrated that crime had yet to be reduced appreciably, even though he and his team had only been in office a few months.

Not long after, I sat down for a breakfast meeting with Daniel at a restaurant near the Inner Harbor. The meeting was ostensibly to discuss union concerns. But Daniel was in a foul mood that day, and I quickly found out why.

Martin was hell-bent on bringing a form of CompStat—now rebranded as Citi-Stat—to all of the city's municipal bureaus. An article in that morning's *Sun*, in fact, had noted that the Department of Public Works was about to implement aspects of the innovative tracking system. And Martin, in an off-hand remark to the reporter, had said something like: If DPW can do it, I don't know why the police department can't.

Daniel, of course, took it as a veiled shot at his agency—and a not-so-veiled shot at him personally. He was 100 percent right, too. This wasn't something he should have had to read in the newspaper.

Ron was a gentleman. A straight arrow. I don't ever remember him cussing, which was, as you can imagine, unusual for a cop. But he was clearly frustrated now. With me as a captive audience, he launched into a mini-rant about the mistreatment he'd been receiving from the man he kept referring to as "Your mayor."

Not *his* mayor.

Not *our* mayor.

Suddenly, it was *your* mayor.

"I wonder what they'd do if I quit?" he said gloomily.

"I don't know what they'd do, sir," I replied, hoping to buck up his spirits. "But we'd be very disappointed."

After that conversation, I felt the need to walk up to City Hall. There, I asked to see Michael Enright, Martin's Chief of Staff. As we talked, the mayor popped in and asked: "What's going on?"

I explained that I had just come from a meeting with Ron Daniel, and there were vast storm clouds—metaphorically speaking—on the horizon.

"Martin," I said, "you can't be talking to the commissioner through the newspaper. He didn't take it well."

The mayor stared at me and said: "I don't care how he took it."

Ohhh-kay. And that was basically the end of *that* conversation.

Leaving there, I walked over to Police Headquarters. My plan now was to tell Daniel: "Hey, let this one go, OK? Don't bring it up with Martin." Because I knew, with the over-heated emotions on both sides, if the two were to meet that morning, only one would walk out of there with a job.

But Ron wasn't in his office. I left a message for him to call, but I didn't hear from him that day. And the next day I went to Chicago for a national FOP meeting, hoping things would settle down between the two men while I was gone.

Maybe I'd sit down with the two when I got back, do my best Dr. Phil impersonation and help them see the error of their ways and mend fences. But it didn't exactly work out that way.

When I checked into my hotel in Chicago, there was a

message waiting for me from my office. "The mayor's trying to get a hold of you," it said.

Uh-oh. This didn't sound good.

When I finally reached him later in the afternoon, Martin was blunt. "I'm firing your police commissioner," he said.

Again with the *your*!

Your mayor.

Your police commissioner.

Was I getting blamed for all this? For supporting Martin after he won the election? For approving of Ron as the new police commissioner?

Jesus! It was making me more than a little paranoid.

It was here, in mid-conversation with the mayor, that I made a tactical mistake.

"I'm in Chicago," I told him. "Do you want me to come back?"

"Do what you think is best," the mayor replied.

Which of course is the kind of answer your mother would give, leaving you to twist in the wind, frozen with indecision and yet certain that if you *didn't* choose the right option— whatever *that* was—you'd be met with simmering disapproval.

And possibly burn in hell.

So I never unpacked my bag. Instead, I flew back to Baltimore that evening. When I got home around 11, I called Martin.

"We're having a press conference tomorrow," he said, "and I'd like you to be there."

I was stunned. Obviously, in just 24 hours, events had moved along at warp-speed on the Ron Daniel front. A story broke in the *Sun* that Ron had agreed to resign after just 57 days as the police commissioner, ending, the newspaper said, "a contentious reign in which he refused to back the mayor's plan to fight crime."

Quoting unnamed City Hall sources, the paper reported: "When the Maple/Linder group offered 87 suggestions for how to reduce crime in Baltimore, Daniel rejected half." At the same time, other sources were telling the paper that Ed Norris would be named acting police commissioner.

Frankly, I thought this was nuts. Sure, I thought Martin's plan all along was to eventually make Norris the commissioner. But naming him less than two months after Daniel took the job? Uh-uh. I didn't think Martin would have the support of the City Council to put a white guy from New York in charge so soon.

But I knew Martin well enough at this point to know none of that really mattered. Martin was gonna do what Martin was gonna do. And I had to support him.

"Mayor O'Malley has a mandate to reduce crime and do it now," I told reporters. "Apparently his plans on how to accomplish this are different from Commissioner Daniel's."

When I got to City Hall the next morning for the presser and went up to the mayor's office, things got even more sur-real. I found Martin pacing about wearing—this was a sight I will never un-see—a firefighter's helmet with the ear flaps pulled down and a baseball glove.

He was also gripping a baseball.

I wondered if he had lost his mind.

The explanation, however, proved far more mundane: he was scheduled to throw out the first pitch at the Orioles' season-opener at Camden Yards in a few days. So now he was practicing his throws with Mike Enright. (Don't ask why Martin wore a fire helmet. I never learned the answer.)

In a matter of minutes, I was subbing in for Enright and playing catch with the mayor. At this point, I should mention we were doing it surrounded by what appeared to be expensive paintings from the Walters Art Museum on loan to the mayor's office.

I should also mention it was a good thing that throwing a baseball was not needed in Martin's line of work, because the whole concept of step-with-the-left-foot, throw-with-the-right seemed to elude him.

All I could think about was him bouncing a throw off one of the beautiful works of art that lined the walls. And I envisioned the curator of the Walters having a heart attack when informed there was now a hole roughly 9 ½ inches in circumference in said artwork that corresponded nicely to the size of a regulation Rawlings baseball.

Luckily, none of Martin's throws were that wild. Disaster was averted.

The press conference again demonstrated why Martin was such a masterful politician. Facing the first major crisis of his short time in office, and one that touched on the third rail of race in this segregated city, he surrounded himself with nine City Council members, most of them African-Americans.

A front-page photo in the *Sun* the next morning would also show me standing with this group, directly next to the mayor, hands folded demurely in front of me, looking attentive. Also in the photo was Rick Hite, the president of the Vanguard Justice Society, the organization representing Baltimore's black police officers, thus assuring an anxious populace that the city's two police unions were squarely behind the young mayor on the Ron Daniel contretemps.

"This has been the toughest decision that I have ever had

to make and one that caused me a great deal of personal sadness," Martin told the assembled media. Yet, he went on: "I
promised the people of this city that we will make it safer."

The grumbling from much of the city's African-American
community over Ron Daniel's sudden departure and Ed Norris'
ascension as acting commissioner would go on for months. But
by rallying his political supporters and reiterating to the cops
that this was the dawning of a new law and order regime, Martin
had successfully defused a potentially explosive situation.

Clearly, though, the mayor's honeymoon period was over.
I felt sorry for Daniel, a good and decent man who didn't
deserve his fate. But the prospect of working for Ed Norris,
even on an acting basis, had invigorated the entire police
department.

Despite my initial doubts, I knew Martin would lobby
hard to make Ed the permanent commissioner, and he did.
With Norris in tow, he launched another patented O'Malley
charm offensive with multiple appearances in front of the City
Council, in heated town hall meetings throughout the city,
even in front of the state delegation in Annapolis.

And of course it worked.

In late spring, Norris was unanimously confirmed as the
new commissioner by the City Council. And a few weeks
later, he was officially sworn in during a ceremony at the War
Memorial Building, where he received a standing ovation.

In the weeks and months that followed, with his relentless
enthusiasm, with his appearances at crime scenes all over the
city at all hours, and with his unwavering support of his officers, Ed Norris breathed life into a demoralized police force.

One thing above all else was clear: we were no longer
being led by "a social worker with a gun."

25.

The Carnage Takes Its Toll

Yet a year that started with such high hopes quickly turned into months of anguish as we suffered a shocking wave of police officers killed on the job.

For me, it began when Baltimore County Sgt. Bruce A. Prothero, working off-duty as a security guard in a Pikesville jewelry store, was killed during a robbery in February. It was not unusual for those of us in the BPD to offer our help when a county officer went down, and the county cops would do the same for us when the situation was reversed. Besides, I was still the national trustee from Maryland for the FOP and felt a moral obligation to assist.

So when Martin O'Malley expressed interest in attending the upcoming Prothero funeral—it would be his first police funeral as chief executive—I offered to work out the logistics and go with him.

The Prothero killing was heart-wrenching for everyone. Bruce was 35, a decorated 12-year veteran who was married with five young children, including triplets. He was also only the fifth officer to die in the line of duty—by virtue of the fact he was in uniform and took police action to stop the robbers— in that department's 126-year-history.

During the robbery, two men had entered the store, flashed a gun and grabbed some jewelry before fleeing. When Prothero chased the robbers outside, he was shot as they ran to a getaway car in the parking lot. Gravely wounded, the sergeant was taken to Sinai Hospital, where he died a few hours later.

On the ride from City Hall to the two-hour service at Reisterstown United Methodist Church, and then during the miles-long funeral procession to Dulaney Valley Memorial Gardens in Timonium, I had the new mayor all to myself in his chauffeured car.

Despite the aching sadness of the occasion, I was not above a bit of shameless lobbying for the men and women in blue that I represented. I say a "bit" of lobbying, but I'm sure Martin felt I was wearing him out with my non-stop talk about the city's new crime plan and the urgent need for a new contract for Baltimore's cops.

Martin and I, it must be said, were not on the same wavelength on the contract. His argument to me was: you cops reduce crime, more people move back into the city, this increases the tax base and I'll be able to pay you more. Which meant our officers would have to wait for raises. Uh-uh. That wasn't going to work for us.

My argument was: you pay us *and* we'll reduce crime. I'm going to make sure we do it. Ed Norris, our kick-ass new commissioner, will make sure we do it. But in the meantime, you give our officers a shot in the arm with a good contract. Meaning sooner rather than later.

I won't pretend I was able to change Martin's mind on any of this. But being stuck in a massive funeral cortege with Baltimore's new leader was not the worst thing that could happen to a police union president.

It also proved to be a nice bonding experience; by the time the traffic allowed us to leave the cemetery for the ride back to City Hall, we were down to talking about our wives and kids and whether the Orioles could improve on their crappy fourth-place finish of the previous year.

A month later, the first of the BPD tragedies occurred when Officer Jamie A. Roussey died after his cruiser crashed into another car in West Baltimore. He had sped through an intersection trying to reach three fellow officers chasing a man suspected of marijuana possession. (The man was also found to have a Glock 9 mm handgun and drug paraphernalia in the trunk of his car.)

This was an especially devastating loss for the department. Roussey was only 22, and came from a family with a long legacy in the BPD. His father, Fred, his brother, Fred Jr., an uncle and a cousin were all cops. The cousin, Seth Roussey, had been the first officer on the scene of the accident. And the uncle, Vincent Roussey, was part of the mayor's security detail.

When I met Fred Roussey in the hallway at Shock Trauma that day, he was in tears and the two of us could only hug. But as I told reporters later, as devastated as Fred was, he was also immensely proud of his son.

"Most fathers want their sons to follow in their footsteps," I said. "(Jamie) was such a young guy who really wanted to make a difference."

What I didn't add is that if you're a parent of a cop, you're also scared to death every moment of the day for your son or daughter, knowing how dangerous the job is in a city like Baltimore.

There was, as you can imagine, another huge police funeral for Jamie Roussey, yet this one was different in a significant way. When you have a young officer killed in the line of duty, you also have a bunch of young cops—his friends, his co-workers, the people in his police academy class —who have never dealt with something like this before, have never experienced the overwhelming shock and grief that comes with a cop's death.

Coming face-to-face with this kind of emotional turmoil when, in many cases, these young people are just a few years removed from their carefree high school days, is a sobering reminder of the perils of their new profession.

Some six weeks after we lost Jamie Roussey, Officer Kevon Gavin was killed in another horrendous car crash. Kevon had pulled his cruiser into West Lombard Street to block the path of a 17-year-old behind the wheel of Ford Bronco, who was being pursued by police after he opened fire with a 10 mm handgun while wearing body armor on a Baltimore street corner.

The Bronco was thought to be traveling at nearly 100 mph when it collided with Kevon's vehicle, landing on top, crushing the roof and igniting a fire. Rushed to Shock Trauma, he died a day later, on Good Friday.

Gavin, 27, was a combat veteran of the Persian Gulf War and had been on the police force for six years. He was married with a 15-month-old son and two stepchildren, ages 5 and

8. And this, of course, was another heart-wrenching police funeral at which Martin O'Malley was pressed once again into being the Comforter-in-Chief.

But in remarks to the media before the service, the mayor couldn't help expressing his own shock and frustration at the senseless manner in which Kevon was killed, and the bleak circumstances that led another lost young man on the streets of Baltimore to pull out a gun.

"When I was 17," Martin said sadly, "I was just glad to have the keys to the car. I didn't put on a bulletproof vest when I went out for the night."

"We cannot accept what has happened," the mayor said later inside the funeral home, just feet from where an honor guard stood a somber watch over Kevon's casket.

Yet in a sense, acceptance is exactly what ended up happening in this case. At his trial, the young gunman whose actions had precipitated the horrific crash was acquitted of all charges, including first-degree murder, vehicular manslaughter, transportation of a handgun and wearing a bullet-proof vest.

The verdict, of course, was a real kick in the teeth to the men and women of the police force, a sign that the people who lived and worked in the city and whose lives we had sworn to protect and serve, would not back us up.

As the months went on, the death toll in the BPD kept rising.

In October, Sgt. John D. Platt, 35, and Officer Kevin McCarthy, 36, were broadsided in their cruiser by a pickup truck that blew past a stop sign and barreled through an intersection. The driver had been drinking and doing over 60 mph in a 25-mph speed zone, and the force of the crash was such that it slammed the cruiser into a telephone pole.

By the time the officers were cut from their car, both were dead. Platt, a 17-year veteran of the force, had a wife, a three-year-old son and a four-year-old daughter. McCarthy, on the force 15 years, had a nine-year-old daughter.

Both deaths were horrific, of course. But what made Platt's even more wrenching for the rank and file was that he was remembered as the officer into whose arms Lt. Owen Sweeney had collapsed three years earlier after being shot in the back by a mentally unstable man.

We knew the pain of that terrible event—when Sweeney and Platt answered a call from a woman whose husband was off his meds and acting erratically—had never really left the sergeant. And now his family would have to endure the same searing grief Elaine Sweeney and her two sons were *still* enduring.

In any event, the police department now had a double funeral to prepare for. The two officers had been great friends and their families wanted a single service for both to be held at Lassahn Funeral Home in Overlea.

Massive crowds descended there to pay their respects; thousands of police officers stood vigil outside, since only a few hundred mourners could fit inside. Predictably, it was a day of tears and gut-wrenching sorrow that left so many of us empty and exhausted once again.

The only light moment I can remember occurred when Martin O'Malley, his wife Katie and their young son, Will, arrived for the evening viewing. Commissioner Ed Norris and I were standing outside when the mayor's car pulled up, and we both noticed Martin was wearing a badge with a black mourning band around it.

This was considered a big no-no for a civilian. The department had given Martin a ceremonial badge after he was sworn in. But badges with mourning bands are to be worn only by cops at a police funeral.

"Tell your mayor he shouldn't wear that," Ed said to me.

Here we go again with the YOUR mayor stuff, I thought.

"No," I replied, *"you* tell *your* boss he shouldn't wear it."

But finally I relented. I went up to Martin, shook his hand, pulled him in close and said: "Hey, appreciate you wearing the badge, but the guys will take it wrong. You should probably take it off."

Informed of the faux pas, Martin quickly did the right thing. A minute or so later, when Ed joined us, Martin said: "Yeah, McLhinney told me to take the badge off."

In perfect deadpan, Norris looked at me and said: "Why'd you have him do that?"

The old saying is true: sometimes you have to laugh to keep from crying. And let me tell you, there sure as hell aren't too many chuckles at a police funeral.

The terrible spate of fallen police officers continued into the following year, 2001.

In March, Officer Michael J. Cowdery was shot and killed outside a Chinese carryout in East Baltimore. He and his three partners were in plainclothes with their police badges hanging from their necks, when they stopped to question two men who looked like drug dealers.

As Cowdery talked with a woman who had just left the carryout, a man brandishing a silver .357 magnum approached and shot the officer below his left knee. When Cowdery collapsed screaming on the sidewalk, the assailant held the gun to his head and shot him again.

One of Cowdery's partners then got in a running gun-battle with the shooter, who took five bullets to his legs before he was finally subdued. Forty packets of cocaine were found in his pockets. A jury would go on to found him guilty of first-degree murder.

Cowdery was 31 when he was killed. On the force a little over three years, he left behind his parents, sister and a son. His father, Michael J. Cowdery Sr., was a Philadelphia police detective who had inspired his son to follow in his footsteps. So here again was another grim entry in the chronicle of law enforcement dads who welcome their sons on the job only to have their worst nightmares come true.

Mercifully, there was a lull in the wave of these departmental tragedies until August of 2002, when Officer Crystal Sheffield died after her cruiser collided with an unmarked police car in West Baltimore as both rushed to help a fellow officer.

The 35-year-old Sheffield thus became city's first female police officer killed in the line of duty, another grim milestone for the department. By all accounts, she loved her job and her death hit the BPD hard. The mother of an 11-year-old boy and the wife of a Baltimore fire lieutenant, she also had a brother, sister and brother-in-law in the police department.

As Ed Norris would note, Crystal was the sixth officer to be killed on the job since he took over as commissioner. Her death continued another disturbing trend, too: she was the fourth of those cops to die in a car crash.

Less than three months later, the department was rocked again when another officer was killed, a murder Commissioner Norris would label the most brutal of his tenure.

In the early morning hours of Nov. 23, Detective Thomas

G. Newman was shot and killed in what was described as "a flat-out execution" outside a bar in Dundalk.

As the 37-year-old officer left Joe's Tavern with his girlfriend near closing time, two men approached and, without a word, opened fire. After Tommy fell to the ground, the gunmen stood over him and continued shooting.

As Norris recounted in his 2017 memoir, "Way Down in the Hole," after Tommy Newman died, a doctor in the operating room showed him the detective's heart.

"The sight shook me as few others had," Norris wrote. "The heart had four bullets sticking straight out of it. Which meant someone had stood directly over his fallen body to pump the last few shots that had ended his life."

Detective Newman's killers fled, but they were arrested later that day. Police soon learned the officer was murdered in retaliation for testifying against two men who had shot and wounded him a year earlier after a confrontation at a gas station.

Tommy Newman, the father of a six-year-old son and a three-year-old daughter, had pushed through a long and painful recovery from his injuries to return to work, earning the respect and admiration of his fellow officers. This was a good, aggressive and steadfast cop, like all the rest mentioned here, gone way too soon from this world.

A few nights after Tommy was murdered, his family, friends, co-workers and community members held a candlelight vigil in the parking lot where he was gunned down. As the tears flowed and speakers spoke words of loss and grief and comfort, I couldn't help thinking this would be the last time I'd be representing the brave men and women of the Baltimore City Police Department.

Years of burying friends and consoling families, and fighting tooth and nail in the FOP for my cops, had taken its toll on me.

A new job opportunity seemed to be presenting itself. And I was eager to see if it was a good fit.

If nothing else, I thought, stepping away from the carnage in Baltimore would do wonders for my mental health.

26.

The Hidden Gem of Law Enforcement

It would be yet another combative election, this one for governor of Maryland in 2002, that would ultimately spur me to leave the best job I'd ever had: representing the men and women of the Baltimore Police Department who put their lives on the line every day.

By the spring of that year, I'd been approached by the campaigns of Kathleen Kennedy Townsend, the presumptive Democratic nominee, and Robert L. Ehrlich Jr., the Republican front-runner, both hoping for the FOP's endorsement.

Even then, I leaned toward supporting Ehrlich. I had gotten to know Bob a few years earlier when he'd invited me to Richmond, Va. to look at Project Exile. This was a program designed to reduce that city's homicide rate by detaining violent handgun offenders and prosecuting them in federal court, where they'd face a mandatory five-year minimum sentence in federal prison.

I'd come away impressed with the program, one which *really* went after criminals. I was also taken with the young, four-term congressman from the 2nd Congressional District who struck me as affable, down-to-earth and a true friend of law enforcement.

I related to Bob on a personal level, too. He'd grown up in a working class family in Arbutus, but was talented enough in football to play for Gilman, the prestigious private school in Baltimore, and Princeton University, where he was the team's co-captain.

Also influencing my support for Ehrlich was this: I had gotten wind that Mayor Martin O'Malley wasn't thrilled with KKT. She had been the lieutenant governor under Parris Glendening for eight years and was also a big friend of police. But her criticism of Ed Norris' decision to downsize Hotspot, a program she'd championed that provided money for crime-fighting—including social work and drug treatment in high-crime areas—irritated the hell out of O'Malley. Not to mention his new police commissioner, who was on a roll and garnering nationwide notice for lowering the city's homicide rate.

"I'm puzzled why any thinking person would question the deployment decisions of the most successful police chief in the country right now," Martin told the *Sun* in a not-so-subtle dig at his fellow Democrat.

Reading those words, you could almost envision little puffs of steam coming from the mayor's ears and the top of his head about to explode.

Martin, in fact, asked me to take a shot at KKT—a figurative one, obviously. I did this in a letter in which I accused her of "political grandstanding" on the Hotspot issue. The letter was soon tactically leaked to the media by the FOP at the request of O'Malley's staff, and a big story about it appeared in the newspaper.

My comments must have come across as scathing. Because I soon got a call from the mayor in which he chuckled and said: "I told you to take a *shot*, not shoot her between the eyes."

In the past 35 years, the FOP had never endorsed a Republican for governor. But I sensed that was about to change. Sure enough, our membership voted overwhelmingly to support Bob Ehrlich —even though the state FOP endorsed KKT. From that point on, we were all in for him, raising money through a PAC fund, providing an FOP car for his use and uniformed officers for his TV commercials.

When Rudy Giuliani, then at the height of his post-911 popularity, came to town for an Ehrlich campaign event, we even let his Hizzoner's helicopter land on the roof of Police Headquarters.

Good thing Martin never found out about that stunt. He would have gone batshit crazy.

On Election Night, I joined other FOP members on stage with Ehrlich after his decisive win over KKT ended a 36-year losing streak by Republican gubernatorial candidates.

"By toppling a Kennedy in a state dominated by Democratic voters," the *Sun* wrote, "Ehrlich's victory made good on the symbolism of his campaign: that a working-class kid could, against all odds, beat a privileged member of America's most stories political family."

So I was not exactly surprised a couple of days later when I received word that the governor-elect wanted to talk to me.

I knew a job offer might be in the wind, and I was ready

to listen. I had served as FOP president just shy of 10 years, five election terms, the longest-serving president in its history. You can't stay too long in these jobs, I knew. I was ready for a change. And with 22 ½ years in the police department, I could leave and collect my pension.

When Bob and I sat down, he got right to the point. "What would you like to do in the administration?" he asked.

I had been giving this a good deal of thought and had sought counsel from Paul Schurick, Ehrlich's campaign director, as well as my inner circle at the FOP.

"I'd like to show that a good guy can run a police department," I answered.

In retrospect, it was a bold statement from an officer who had never held rank. True, I had led a large organization that represented thousands of cops. But that was a completely different animal.

"What agency are you looking at?" Bob asked.

"The MDTA," I told him.

The Maryland Transportation Authority police force was the hidden gem of state law enforcement, as far as I was concerned. It generated its own revenue and wasn't dependent on the state budget, which made it an enticing place to land for a new leader determined to raise the agency's profile and instill in it a greater sense of purpose.

With more than 450 sworn officers and some 200 civilian professionals, the MDTA was responsible for policing the state's bridges, tunnels and toll roads, as well as Baltimore/Washington International Airport and the Port of Baltimore. After the devastating Sept. 11 terrorist attacks on New York and Washington D.C., protecting these assets became an even more urgent matter than before.

A few days later, Bob agreed to my request. Ed Norris was also looking to leave the BPD after a series of run-ins with the mayor and his staff over what he perceived to be their micro-managing of his job. Ed was also catching heat for an off-the-books departmental fund that had recently come to light, and Ehrlich was soon courting him, too.

So it was that in late December, the new administration's law enforcement team was announced to great fanfare.

Ed Norris was named the new Superintendant of the Maryland State Police, a move that stunned city officials, who lauded him (rightly) for the 28 percent drop in violent crime over the past three years. I was named the new MDTA Police Chief. And Douglas DeLeaver, the former MTA Police Chief, was named head of the Department of Natural Resources Police.

Heading up the state's eighth-largest law enforcement agency, I would tell people, was every cops dream job. But my sense was that this was an agency that needed to work more than it was allowed to. I had friends there who confirmed they felt under-used and under-valued.

I vowed to change that mind-set from the get-go. And to a large extent, we did.

In my four years running the department, drunken driving arrests rose 40 percent. Traffic citations rose 54 percent, drug arrests by a whopping 207 percent and criminal arrests by 100 percent.

Maybe this was the statistic that was most meaningful— and the one I was most proud of: handgun arrests increased 1000 percent. Keeping weapons out of the hands of bad guys was perhaps the single best thing we could do to keep the citizens of Maryland safe.

I hit the ground running in my new job. We made sure everyone else on the force was keeping up, too.

And it was in this energized, pedal-to-the-metal atmosphere that I'd soon face—by far—my biggest challenge as chief.

27.

A Rumor of Destruction

It started with an ominous phone call from the FBI in October of 2005. And it would end with international news coverage of an event that thrust Maryland into the growing conversation about how cities protect themselves in a post-911 world.

"We have a credible threat of a terrorist plot to bomb one of the Baltimore tunnels," said the agent who called me.

At a briefing later at the FBI field office in Woodlawn, I was told many of the details of the plot were still vague. There was, for example, no specific info on when this would happen. Or whether the target was the Fort McHenry Tunnel, which carries traffic on I-95 beneath the city's harbor, or the Harbor Tunnel, which conveys I-895 traffic under the Patapsco River southeast of downtown.

We also weren't told who was involved in the plot. The fact that more information wasn't forthcoming didn't surprise me. As I knew from prior experience, the FBI doesn't tell you everything they know—just what they *think* you should know.

All we would learn from the bureau's Special Agent in Charge, Kevin Perkins, was that they'd received a tip from a source in a European country that men of Egyptian origin, including one living in Baltimore, were behind the plot.

According to the tipster, the plan called for a box truck full of explosives to be driven into the tunnel. The driver would then be picked up by a confederate before the explosives were detonated. *Or* the driver would go up with the truck, achieving a form of sick martyrdom most rational people will never understand.

The plotters were under surveillance, Perkins reported, and an operation to arrest them before they could strike was underway.

My reaction to all this, which I thought was fairly rational at the time, was: "What happens if you don't get them all?"

The answer was chilling: "Then it'll be to you to protect the tunnels."

As daunting as that task was, it was not as if we were totally unprepared for it. In the wake of Sept. 11, 2001, we had thought long and hard about how to keep the tunnels safe from terrorist attacks.

We had done burn exercises where we closed the tunnels early on Saturday mornings and set ablaze a 55-gallon oil drum to test the ventilation system. We had had structural engineers do an assessment of the amount of explosives it would take to breach the tunnels and cause them to flood.

We had done drills, looked at plans, done both live and tabletop exercises to plan for every threat imaginable. Yet what was facing us now was no longer in the realm of imagination.

This was a specific threat—or at least thought to be. And we had roughly two days before the FBI planned to take enforcement action that might—or might not—end the threat. So I went back to MDTA headquarters and worked all night with my team to come up with ways to prevent a possible catastrophe.

The logistics were formidable. Both tunnels were about a mile and a half long. Our operational people came up with a plan for using trucks full of sand to block the four entrances and exits on each side of the Fort McHenry Tunnel, and the two on each side of the Harbor Tunnel. Trucks with impact attenuators—also known as crash cushions—would be set up to reduce the damage to the tunnels' structure in the event of a vehicle crash.

Closing the tunnels was one thing. But then what would we do with the traffic? I-95 is the nation's longest north-south interstate highway, running over 1900 miles from Maine to Florida. Some 115,000 vehicles flow through the eight lanes of the Fort McHenry Tunnel on an average day, with 71,000 using the four-lane Harbor Tunnel. Shutting both down would create a traffic nightmare; we needed a plan to avert this, too.

There was no way we could warn motorists about a possible closure ahead of time, either. That would attract a ton of media attention and a slew of questions from city officials demanding to know what the hell was going on. All of which could tip off the bad guys.

Underscoring the seriousness of the challenge before us, as we were spit-balling scenarios for dealing with wild-eyed jihadists in a bomb-laden truck, one of my commanders used the term "acceptable casualties."

I have to admit that shook me.

Wow! I thought. *Acceptable casualties! That's a military term! That's not something civilian law enforcement talks about!* He was talking about which tactical plan would result in the least amount of carnage, not how to *avoid* the carnage altogether.

All sorts of other alarming scenarios floated in my head. If we were successful in closing the tunnel before the box truck got in, we'd essentially be leaving it in the midst of a massive traffic tie-up.

What kind of orders do I give my officers then?

Shoot the driver?

Talk about *another* situation law enforcement doesn't normally face...

Or do we somehow clear the tunnel, allow the truck entry, and let the terrorists blow up their cargo? Sure, that would eliminate any casualties—aside from the occupants themselves, of course, now presumably bound for paradise in a thousand tiny pieces for their rendezvous with the fabled 72 virgins.

But obviously the slight flaw in *that* plan was it would create a massive explosion and major infrastructure damage that would take months, if not years, to repair. Preventing mass civilian injury and death, though, was always our main concern.

So a day and a half before the feds were to take down the suspected terrorists, we quietly pre-staged teams of medics at each end of all the tubes.

This was done around 3 in the morning. We let our cops know what was going on; I trusted them to keep their mouths shut. But we told our guys in operations that this was part of a drill. And then we went out with sand trucks and timed, to the minute, how long it would take to shut each tunnel down.

The night before the FBI was to begin its operation, I briefed the governor on what was to go down. I really learned something about Bob Ehrlich that night. You never really know how your boss is going to react in times of extreme stress, especially when something as preposterous as this is dropped in his lap.

But Bob completely trusted us. He asked important questions, as you'd expect any competent chief executive to do. But he didn't second-guess a single thing we were doing.

On the other hand, I knew if our plan went south and something calamitous happened, it would be on me and not the governor. My command staff and I were going to live or die with what happened in the next 12-plus hours.

I didn't get much sleep that night. No check that, I didn't get *any* sleep, my mind racing as I went over every nightmare eventuality I could envision.

The next morning, Oct. 18th, we set up a command center at our headquarters in eastern Baltimore County, at the foot of the Key Bridge. The plan now was this: once we got word the FBI was executing its searches, we would shut down the tunnels in both directions. And once we got the all-clear signal, meaning that everyone implicated in the plot had been captured, we'd re-open them.

Around 11:30, after learning the FBI was on the move, we gave the signal to close both tubes, which was done quickly. Traffic was diverted to the Beltway, with electronic road signs now activated up and down the East Coast, warning motorists of tunnel closures and to expect delays. We also had officers with bomb-sniffing dogs searching suspicious vehicles, particularly tractor-trailers and box trucks.

Within minutes, news helicopters began circling and reporters were calling me to find out the cause of the closures. I kept putting them off. The FBI was now questioning suspects at a market in Highlandtown that specialized in Middle Eastern food, and two Baltimore County pizza restaurants, and the agents needed time to conduct their operation.

Soon enough, the shutdowns and widespread gridlock were attracting national and even international news coverage. But at a little after 1:30, after hearing from the FBI, we reopened the Fort McHenry Tunnel. The Harbor Tunnel was opened a few minutes later.

Except for the snarled traffic and the lingering curses from motorists that would last for hours, the drama was effectively over. Yet it had easily been one of the most trying and frenzied days of my career.

At a news conference later that afternoon, the FBI's Kevin Perkins told reporters that, ultimately, no evidence collected by his agents had corroborated the threat to the tunnels. Nevertheless, I considered the joint federal, state and local operation to be a huge success. We had shut down two major arteries in one of the busiest traffic corridors in the country with zero casualties, all while an important anti-terrorist investigation was taking place.

There was no need for apologies to anyone inconvenienced. We had all done our jobs well.

"We will *always* err on the side of public safety," I told the media.

In the coming days, we would hear an astounding revelation from the FBI. The tunnel threat, it turned out, had its origins in nothing more than an overseas domestic squabble.

Apparently an inmate in a prison in Belgium had learned that his wife was secretly carrying on with a Baltimore man. Hoping to get the paramour out of the picture, the inmate had dropped a dime on him to the Belgian authorities and concocted the tunnel-bombing story.

Only when the FBI flew to Belgium and polygraphed the cuckolded prisoner was the true absurdity of the scheme revealed.

As I said many times throughout my long career in law enforcement: you couldn't make this stuff up.

28.

A Career Comes to a Close

In my five terms as FOP president, I came face-to-face with pain and loss too many times.

I shed too many tears with the families of fallen police officers. I hugged too many distraught wives and moms and dads, brothers and sisters. I watched too many of them crumple in the halls of Shock Trauma after an ashen-faced surgeon broke the awful news that their loved one would not be coming home that night.

I organized too many cop funerals, listened to too many plaintive eulogies, left too many cemeteries feeling numb inside and wondering if my staff and I had done all we could for the "survivors" whose lives would be forever changed.

In my four years as the MDTA police chief, I would go on to lose three officers. Yet with each of these deaths, I would come to know a different kind of pain and loss.

The realization of this first dawned on me in July of 2004, when Officer Duke G. Aaron III was killed after a pickup truck crashed into his unmarked cruiser on the shoulder of Rte. 50 near the Bay Bridge.

Duke was pretty much dead at the scene. He had just issued a citation to a driver and returned to his car to finish the paperwork when he was hit. The high-speed rear-end collision was so violent that the trunk and bumper of his car were pushed all the way into the driver's compartment.

The driver of the pickup, a 32-year-old from Queenstown named Albert Gene Antonelli, was found to be under the influence of several drugs and driving on a suspended license, with a host of traffic violations in his past as well as arrests on drug possession charges.

The MDTA police were not used to line-of-duty deaths, and so the loss of Officer Aaron was devastating for the department. As I drove to the bridge immediately after the accident to meet with our officers and civilian staff and attempt to console them and thank them for their professionalism—in the midst of their shock and grief, they still had to coordinate the crime scene and handle all their other duties—I was surprised by the emotions I felt.

This death shook me in a different way from the ones I'd witnessed in the BPD. For the first time, *I* was the guy in charge when an officer went down. It was a sobering reminder of my new responsibilities.

Here was a young cop doing what *I* asked these men and women to do every day, which was to go out there and be aggressive in enforcing the laws and protecting motorists.

Duke was our top-performing officer at the Bay Bridge. He had written more tickets and been part of more investigations than any other officer. Weeks earlier, he had climbed out onto the bridge to save a woman who was threatening to jump into the waters of the Chesapeake Bay. Yet in the blink of an eye, Duke's own life had been cut short in the most awful way.

The Bay Bridge is a particularly dangerous area, and a tough place to police from a traffic standpoint. There's no room for error. Yet officers like Duke Aaron, a rising star at 29 and a three-time Officer of the Year, did the hazardous work without complaint, knowing it must be done to save lives.

A year later in July, our department was rocked again by another tragedy, this one the death of Grant Turner. Grant, 24, was a recruit in our police academy. He was just weeks from graduating when he collapsed in front of his classmates after taking part in—ironically—an FOP 5K race to honor Duke Aaron. (Grant's death would later be traced to a heart defect.)

I was on vacation in western Maryland when I heard the news, and I raced back to be with Grant's family. I had known his dad, who had been an Annapolis cop and a member of the Anne Arundel Sheriff's Department. To make Grant's death even more lamentable, I learned he had been engaged to be married in two months.

Then and there I vowed that we would elevate Grant to officer status, and that the agency would consider his a departmental line of duty death, meaning he'd be buried with full honors.

Two days later, I visited his academy classmates to assess the emotional and psychological toll Grant's death had taken on them.

Think about it: here was a bunch of young guys in their early 20's who had just watched one of their own die in front of them. The effect of this could not be understated. The bond between trainees at the academy is powerful; one way they endure the rigors of the 20-week program is through the encouragement and support of their fellow recruits, who often become life-long friends.

Now these young people—there were 24 of them—would have to go on with their lives, and their careers, still reeling from the awful event they'd witnessed.

When I got there that morning, I spoke quietly to them for a few minutes. I wanted them to know that we in the agency supported them, and that we understood what they were going through.

Suddenly, I switched gears and asked them to go put on their gym clothes.

"We're going for a run," I said.

If anyone gave me a funny look, or whispered "Wow, the old man has really lost it," I didn't notice. (Of course, that probably wouldn't have helped their prospects for graduation. When the chief gives an order, no matter how inane it sounds, it's best for a trainee to answer: "Yes, sir! A run sounds like a lovely idea!")

Besides, my order didn't exactly come out of left field: every class does a mile-and-a-half training run each morning. So that's what we did, a brisk jog around the academy property to honor and remember Grant, with the class guidon, or flag, waving proudly.

The mood remained somber during the run. I won't pretend it magically lifted their spirits. But I like to think it took their minds off Grant's death, even for a few minutes. Especially now that they had something else to worry about: whether the old guy huffing and puffing in the back of the pack could keep up.

Five months later, on Dec. 21, we had another officer badly injured in a traffic accident. Cpl. Robert T. Krauss was on his motorcycle, escorting a funeral procession in Baltimore, when he was struck by a drunk driver.

Bob was an 18-year-veteran of the MDTA, one of the best of the best, an officer who had won a commendation five years earlier for capturing a bank robbery suspect. In 2001, he had won a Distinguished Service Award for crawling into an over-turned vehicle and aiding the crash victims until paramedics arrived.

And just as with Grant Turner, there was an eerie linkage to Duke Aaron: Bob had been the first officer on the scene when Duke was killed on that dark day near the Bay Bridge in 2004.

Both the Aaron and Krauss accidents were unsettling to me for another reason: both were out of my sphere of experience. Understand, I had been a cop in Baltimore City. Traffic wasn't our specialty. We didn't do a whole lot of enforcement in that regard. And now I was realizing just how deadly our highways had become with this growing proliferation of impaired drivers.

Immediately after the accident, Bob was rushed to Shock Trauma in critical condition. He'd suffered massive injuries - the surgeons were forced to remove a large part of his chest, which left it so exposed he'd end up wearing one of the department's soft body armors for protection.

Nevertheless, after a few anxious weeks, Bob returned home. We were optimistic that he was on the mend, even knowing he faced further surgeries down the line. But on September 1, 2006, less than nine months after the accident, he died on the operating table at Shock Trauma as doctors attempted a complicated procedure to re-build his rib cage.

Once again, we were a department in mourning. As I had for both Duke Aaron and Grant Turner, I delivered the eulogy at Bob Krauss' funeral, my heart heavy with sorrow, little knowing it would be the last police funeral I'd oversee.

Two months later, Martin O'Malley defeated Bob Ehrlich in Maryland's gubernatorial election, signaling my days heading the MDTA Police were numbered. The new governor gets to pick his "guys"—everyone knows how these staffing games work with the change of administrations. And after campaigning and working for Ehrlich for four years, I was definitely no longer one of Martin's "guys."

I felt it was my duty to hang around to help the O'Malley transition team. But soon after Martin took office, I received the dreaded "tap on the shoulder" and the news that my services were no longer required.

Sure, they may not be the equivalent of the Mafia hit, these political blood-lettings and score-settlings. But they can be plenty brutal in their own way. So it was that on January 26, 2007, after sending out an email thanking the hard-working men and women of the MDTA Police for their hard work and dedication the past four years, I officially resigned as their chief.

When reporters asked about my future, I told them I planned to stay in law enforcement.

"I have a lot of opportunities out there," I added.

At that moment, I just wasn't sure what they were.

Epilogue

I did not exactly sit on my rear end after retiring from the MDTA Police.

For eight years, I had the privilege and incredible honor to work for my good friend Herb Weiner, managing partner at the law firm of Schlachman, Belsky and Weiner. Herb and I are like brothers, yet many times he gave me wonderful fatherly advice as well.

Herb's law firm has represented cops and FOP unions since 1966, and I can honestly say several hundred officers owe their careers—and their personal freedom—to Herb and his team of lawyers. I know I do.

While my job at the firm was to bring in new business and work with existing clients, the most enjoyable aspect was negotiating police labor contracts. Herb had taught me a lot over the years. But watching him do battle over police pay and benefits was a sight to see. It confirmed my righteous belief in the saying I'd regularly trot out: "We represented the good guys."

In January 2015, I received a call from another good friend and colleague, Steve Moyer, former lieutenant colonel of the Maryland State Police and second in command under Ed Norris. Steve had been asked by the incoming governor, Larry Hogan, to serve as the Secretary of the Department of Public Safety and correctional Services (DPSCS.) Now Steve wanted to know if I was interested in joining his team.

I really enjoyed working with everyone at SBW Law. But

Steve's come-on was irresistible: "We're getting the band back together for one more run." I couldn't pass up the opportunity to work for the new governor, and especially for Steve.

I started in 2015 as the Director of Professional Standards and Labor Liaison. In 2019, I was promoted to Assistant Secretary for Special Operations. With almost 10,000 employees and over 22,000 inmates and thousands more under its supervision, DPSCS is a beast of a department.

Steve explained that his priority, and Gov. Hogan's, was to root out corruption and correctional officer misconduct in an agency known to have plenty of both.

The department had recently weathered a scandal of historic proportions at the Baltimore City Detention Center, where a detainee named Tavon White, leader of a gang called Black Guerilla Family (BGF) and 40 others, including 24 correctional officers, ran a criminal enterprise involving smuggled contraband and sex between officers and prisoners.

Steve wanted us to develop a plan—and unit—dedicated solely to addressing the corruption issue. The need became even more apparent a few months later with the 2015 Freddie Gray riots in Baltimore and the arrest of two of our employees, who were shown on the evening newscasts looting a neighborhood convenience store.

For the past seven years, our focus has been on stopping the many dishonorable employees willing to smuggle in drugs and cell phones to inmates prepared to pay thousands of dollars for such contraband. Hundreds of correctional officers have been arrested during our administration and almost 100 have been sentenced to years in both state and federal prisons for corruption.

Sadly, I don't believe the problem has abated. It continues

at an alarming rate to this day.

Without a doubt, being a correctional officer is the hardest job in public safety. Being locked up with thousands of murderers, rapists and stick-up boys is no one's idea of an easy gig. Little wonder that there's a saying in corrections: "We only control this prison because they let us."

Yet thankfully, behind the formidable stone walls of these penitentiaries, there are brave men and women willing to put their lives on the line every day to protect the rest of us.

Final Thoughts

Forgive me for beginning on a depressing note: both police leadership and political leadership across Baltimore have not only failed rank-and-file officers, but also the citizens who deserve to be protected and live their lives with some sense of normalcy. Forty years in the business of law enforcement and public safety should lend credibility to that pronouncement.

Without the slightest hesitation, I can state that I've only met a dozen or so cops during my career that entered policing for the wrong reasons. A few were outright racists. A few others were far more heavy-handed with citizens than they needed to be when doing their jobs.

But the vast majority of cops I met and served with were honest and hard-working. These men and women cared mightily about their communities, and were willing to brave a bullet to do a job few others have the courage to do.

In a sense, one must marvel at the biggest political scam perpetrated on the citizens of not just Baltimore, but cities all across the country. It is this: because of failed political and police leadership and an unrelenting barrage of finger-pointing at the actions of individual officers, our elected leaders have somehow managed to convince a large segment of our most vulnerable population that the police are now the bad guys—and that the actions and inactions at City Hall and Police Headquarters have nothing to do with the violent crime crisis in this country.

This is—a more polite colloquialism escapes me at the moment—utter bullshit.

The failure of elected leaders in Baltimore as a whole—from city council members, mayors, prosecutors and on down the line—has directly contributed to what we have now: a city with no immediate and meaningful crime plan to reduce the slaughter of its citizens.

Instead, we have politicians that gaze at the ever-increasing violence and see just numbers. Not sons, husbands, fathers and brothers. Not daughters, wives, mothers and sisters. Just slashes on a tally sheet. Cold statistics, nothing more.

Some so-called leaders want citizens to believe that cities must make a choice between effective policing and constitutional policing. But this is a false choice. Good policing starts with good hiring practices. To attract quality individuals to a department, our leaders first need to stop singling out the actions of a handful of bad cops and claiming this is representative of the over 900,000 police officers in this country.

I have yet to meet a single cop who feels the actions of disgraced Minneapolis police officer Derek Chauvin, convicted of murdering George Floyd in May of 2020, were proper and legal. Yet pandering elected officials will often bring up Floyd's killer to portray *all* police officers in a negative light.

Make no mistake, there are influential elected officials who absolutely believe the police are the enemy of every minority member in this country. Couple that bias with the number of officers ambushed and killed over the past few years and you have to ask: why in God's name would anyone want this job, in this or any other city? No wonder the Baltimore City Police Department is over 600 officers short of its required staffing levels.

The fact is, you can be both pro-police and against police misconduct. You can believe that Blue Lives Matter *and* Black Lives Matter *and* All Lives Matter at the same time. The larger choice comes down to this: are you on the side of law and order? Or on the side of those who willingly prey on the innocent?

Outside of a very few in Baltimore and Maryland, gone are the principled and fearless leaders who know the right path to take in the never-ending fight against crime, regardless of political consequences. Former Police Commissioners Ed Norris and Fred Bealefeld, who led the department from 2007-2012, saved hundreds of lives in Charm City with their no-nonsense policies targeting the most dangerous criminals. Yet both Norris and Bealefeld were called racists for working to make sure our most impoverished neighborhoods were safer.

Governor Bob Ehrlich fought like hell to bring a successful federal program, first implemented in Richmond, Va., to Maryland that would put the worst of our criminals away for a long time. Project Exile worked in other cities—the NRA and the Brady Campaign to Prevent Gun Violence both supported it. Maryland adopted a version of it, but never the whole program, apparently fearing too many young black males would be arrested. Yet Ehrlich, too, was criticized endlessly for his efforts.

One has only to read the report from the Maryland Commission to Restore Trust in Policing, created by the state legislature, to see where poor and corrupt policing has its roots. I was honored to be appointed to the commission by Governor Larry Hogan as one of only two former sworn police officials.

After two years of reviewing thousands of pages of documents and interviewing dozens of witnesses, the commission concluded that the root cause of the Gun Trace Task Force scandal—in 2017, eight members of an elite unit in the BPD were charged in the most shocking corruption scandal in the department's history—was a total lack of supervision, along with senior- level command willfully turning a blind eye to crooked cops.

Shockingly, during a committee hearing, when I asked the current Police Commissioner, Michael Harrison, if the department had done an analysis of how the GTTF scandal could have been avoided, his answer was no. The city's lawyers, he said, felt an analysis might hurt Baltimore's efforts to avoid costly lawsuits. Unbelievable.

As a commission member, it was obvious to me that then-Police Commissioner Kevin Davis chose to focus only on gun seizures, not quality arrests or how officers were getting those weapons off the streets. It was a colossal failure of police leadership. Yet the elected state and local officials chose to completely ignore the findings of a commission they themselves had created. I doubt many of them even bothered to read the final report. When it didn't buy into their political rhetoric, they dismissed it out of hand.

I believe the media has a role in the demoralizing of police agencies, too. A media—especially the TV version of it—that used to believe in "if it bleeds, it leads" now seems to have as its credo "if it's blue, it's bad." Every day the national media seems to scour the country for any negative police encounters it can blow out of proportion. The lies and inaccurate postings about police on social media have contributed mightily to the low morale most departments are experiencing.

Yet this is not a zero-sum situation. We can fix this. A community can have good effective policing where bad guys fear getting arrested and individual rights as spelled out in the U.S. Constitution and Bill of Rights are protected. Those of us who have policed and led police officers know what works and how to make Baltimore—and the nation as a whole—safer.

For starters, cops need to know they're supported. Not just by police leadership, but by the entire criminal justice system. Prosecutors can no longer be seen as the enemies of the men and women in blue, nor the foe of good, solid police work.

Some so-called "reform-minded" prosecutors have determined that they themselves will decide which laws they will or won't enforce. Plain and simple, that is a violation of their oath of office and should result in their immediate dismissal.

Their job is to prosecute criminal cases brought by police agencies—or in some cases, directly by citizens. Elected officials need to step up and impeach anyone in the criminal justice system who refuses to do his or her job.

Judges need to be held more accountable, too. Their sentencing histories for violent offenders need to be part of the public record. Every police officer and prosecutor in Baltimore realizes that defense attorneys shop around in the hope of getting certain—read: more lenient—judges assigned to hear their cases.

Police leadership also needs to be visible and encouraging. This does not mean simply having the mayor or police commissioner stand in front of the TV cameras on occasion to deliver platitudes about an officer's heroics. Every single day, cops do amazing work that needs to be shared by the agencies and praised by the communities. Now that every cop has a body camera, city officials should start posting good arrests on social media, and alerting the TV and print media when they do.

As I've said for years, cops can smell phony a mile away. Any politician or police official who thinks simply showing up at a crime scene or attending roll call is good enough for the troops is sadly mistaken.

Put the damn uniform on, not the dress blues, and hit the streets. (All these years later, I regret not wearing the work uniform as often as I should have.)

A word or two about guns. At the moment, criminals do not fear being caught with a gun. Police across the city and state do not routinely confront criminals in high-crime areas, such as the street corners where they're slinging dope. Make no mistake: all these law-breakers are carrying guns.

Unbelievably, illegal possession of a gun is still a misdemeanor in Maryland. Police departments and communities need to implement a crime plan which focuses on catching bad guys with guns—before they shoot someone. That means aggressively going after criminals on street corners, and after those in cars that troll neighborhoods looking for victims. There needs to be a concerted effort on the part of police leadership and elected officials to devise legal and constitutional tactics to limit the ability of those criminals to freely carry guns.

(And let's not hear anymore from politicians calling for less traffic enforcement. That just gives criminals more places to hide their guns and drugs without fear of being stopped.)

Police also need to focus on serving current arrest warrants and prioritizing the locking up of violent criminals who are known to law enforcement, but are nevertheless currently on the street. This was the strategy employed in New York City under Commissioner Bill Bratton in the mid-1990's and from 2014-2016. The same strategy was used by Ed Norris in Baltimore from 2000 to 2002. This alone will have significant impact on lowering violent crime immediately.

(Regardless of what is said publicly, I know first-hand that the BPD is not prioritizing the serving of warrants and the pursuit of the most violent criminals. In fact, as I type these words, the BPD has eight outstanding warrants for murder currently un-served. And this doesn't take into account the thousands of unsolved shootings and murders in which a suspect has yet to be identified. No wonder people are afraid to come into the city.)

I strongly believe the only ones who should be developing the crime plan for cities like Baltimore are the leaders of the police department and the citizens who live in the communities that now feel under siege. Elected officials should not be involved in crime plan strategizing. If they don't trust those they've hired to run their police department and control crime, then those commanders should be replaced.

If we polled the folks forced to live and work while fearing for their lives, I'd bet my last dollar that they'd support a crime plan that persistently targets violent criminals. And they'd demand that police enforce all the laws that affect their safety and quality of life.

Can you imagine open-air drug markets, or prostitutes being allowed to freely operate in the suburbs? Yet many of our elected officials apparently believe it's OK for poor black folks to live with such scourges.

Finally, police leadership needs to be held accountable for results. And by results, I don't just mean arrests. Bottom line: reducing violent crime and keeping communities safe are the results that matter most. Every day, police commanders should be reviewing crime trends and adjusting their deployment of officers and strategies to reflect those trends.

It's not too late to fix the BPD—and policing in general. Already communities are fighting back and demanding that elected officials make crime-fighting a priority. Only when we elect politicians committed to securing communities and locking up the bad guys will we begin to see substantial change.

In the short term, we need to demand that our elected officials stop blaming the police for the ills of our cities and look in the mirror.

That's where the real blame lies.

Acknowledgments

I wrote this book to honor the brave men and women in the Baltimore Police Department and the Maryland Transportation Authority Police who have sacrificed so much for all of us. I promised their survivors we would "Never Forget." I hope this book helps them realize those were not just words, but something I truly meant from the bottom of my heart.

I especially want to thank Karen Adolfo-Vida, who showed me and the entire City of Baltimore what true sacrifice and courage looks like. And to the everyday heroes, my brothers and sisters in uniform, who answer the call to protect and serve.

Thanks go, of course, to my loving, supportive and encouraging wife, Karen Kruger. And to my sons, Patrick and Danny. The men you have become gives me great joy, and I am so proud of how you lead your lives. Make your mark in this world, and know that I will always love you and be your biggest supporter.

To my Bonus Daughter, Annie Lacher, thank you for allowing me into your life and loving and supporting me throughout your journey to adulthood. So proud of you.

To my father and mother, Jim and Shirley McLhinney, thank you for your example of hard work and sacrifice, and for giving me a solid foundation on which to build my life.

Thanks also to Herb Weiner, my friend and life confidante. Your wise counsel led me to much of the success I've had in life. Not bad for a kid from Violet Avenue. And a kid from Waverly.

Many thanks to Governor Robert L Ehrlich, a man I am fortunate to call my boss and my friend. You believed in me, and my life would never be the same because it. I'm grateful beyond belief to Brad and Charmaine Thomas, co-workers and, most importantly, best friends to both Karen and me. Thanks for your love and support.

Finally, thanks to my co-author, Kevin Cowherd, whose guidance, patience and friendship allowed me to fulfill my promise to our survivors—and to myself.

About the Authors

Gary McLhinney is a retired police officer from the Baltimore City Police Department and former long-term president of the Baltimore Fraternal Order of Police. McLhinney also served as Chief of the Maryland Transportation Authority Police and Assistant Secretary of the Maryland Department of Public Safety and Correctional Services.

He currently operates a consulting business, representing police unions in collective bargaining matters and political strategy.

Kevin Cowherd is the *New York Times* best-selling author of "Hothead" and five other baseball novels for young readers written with Hall of Famer Cal Ripken Jr. Cowherd is also the author of six works of non-fiction. His book, "When the Crowd Didn't Roar: How Baseball's Strangest Game Ever Gave a Broken City Hope" was praised in the *Times*' 2019 Summer Reading Issue as one of the five best new volumes on sports.

Cowherd was an award-winning sports columnist and features writer for the Baltimore *Sun* for 32 years. He has also written for *Men's Health, Parenting* and *Baseball Digest* magazines.

Apprentice House Press

Loyola University Maryland

Apprentice House is the country's only campus-based, student-staffed, full-service book publishing company. Directed by professors and industry professionals, it is a nonprofit activity of the Communication Department at Loyola University Maryland.

Using state-of-the-art technology and an experiential learning model of education, Apprentice House publishes books in untraditional ways. This dual responsibility as publishers and educators creates an unprecedented collaborative environment among faculty and students, while teaching tomorrow's book industry editors, designers, and marketers.

Eclectic and provocative, Apprentice House titles intend to entertain as well as spark dialogue on a variety of topics. Financial contributions to sustain the press's work are welcomed. Contributions are tax deductible to the fullest extent allowed by the IRS.

To learn more about Apprentice House books or to obtain submission guidelines, please visit www.apprenticehouse.com.

Apprentice House Press
Communication Department
Loyola University Maryland
4501 N. Charles Street
Baltimore, MD 21210
410-617-5265
info@apprenticehouse.com
www.apprenticehouse.com